Lucid Dreaming

A Simple Guide to Controlling Dreams While Improving Sleep, Boosting Creativity, Increasing Wellness, and Overcoming Nightmares and Sleep Paralysis

© Copyright 2021

In no way is it legal to reproduce, duplicate, or transmit any part of this document in either electronic means or printed format. Recording of this publication is strictly prohibited, and any storage of this document is not allowed unless with written permission from the publisher. All rights reserved.

The information provided herein is stated to be truthful and consistent, in that any liability, in terms of inattention or otherwise, by any usage or abuse of any policies, processes, or directions contained within is the solitary and utter responsibility of the recipient reader. Under no circumstances will any legal responsibility or blame be held against the publisher for any reparation, damages, or monetary loss due to the information herein, either directly or indirectly.

Respective authors own all copyrights not held by the publisher.

Legal Notice:

This eBook is copyright protected. This is only for personal use. You cannot amend, distribute, sell, use, quote, or paraphrase any part or the content within this eBook without the consent of the author or copyright owner. Legal action will be pursued if this is breached.

Disclaimer Notice:

Please note the information contained within this document is for educational and entertainment purposes only. Every attempt has been made to provide accurate, up-to-date, and reliable complete information. No warranties of any kind are expressed or implied. Readers acknowledge that the author is not engaging in the rendering of legal, financial, medical, or professional advice.

By reading this document, the reader agrees that under no circumstances are we responsible for any losses, direct or indirect, which are incurred as a result of the use of the information contained within this document, including, but not limited to, errors, omissions, or inaccuracies.

Contents

INTRODUCTION 1
LUCID DREAMING ESSENTIALS 4
CHAPTER ONE: THE SCIENCE BEHIND LUCID DREAMING 5
    WHAT IS CONSCIOUSNESS? 6
    INTEGRATED INFORMATION THEORY 7
    THE SCIENCE OF LUCID DREAMING 8
    LANDMARK STUDY ON LUCID DREAMING 9
    LUCID DREAMING IN HISTORY, RELIGION, AND PHILOSOPHY ... 12
    CULTURAL IMPACT 15
CHAPTER TWO: COMMON MISCONCEPTIONS ABOUT LUCID
DREAMING 17
    SHARED LUCID DREAMS 20
    GETTING STUCK IN A DREAM 20
CHAPTER THREE: GETTING PREPARED FOR LUCID DREAMING .. 28
    DREAM JOURNALING 30
    SOME TIPS FOR DREAM JOURNALING 33
START LUCID DREAMING 39
CHAPTER FOUR: BASIC INDUCTION TECHNIQUES 40
    REALITY TESTING 41

- Wake Back to Bed (WBTB) ... 43
- Impossible Movement Practice (IMP) ... 44
- The Counting Technique ... 45
- Mnemonic Induction Lucid Dreaming (MILD) ... 46
- Some Helpful MILD Tips ... 48

CHAPTER FIVE: DREAM CONTROL I: DREAM STABILIZING TECHNIQUES ... 52
- General Guidelines ... 53

CHAPTER SIX: DREAM CONTROL II: GETTING ACCUSTOMED TO YOUR DREAM BODY ... 62
- The Lessons of the Body in Lucid Dreams ... 63
- Preparing Your Body for Lucid Dreaming ... 64
- The Mini-Me Proposal ... 66
- The Lucid Dream Body ... 68
- Reality Checking and the Dream Body ... 69

CHAPTER SEVEN: DREAM OBJECTS AND SYMBOLS ... 72
- Jungian Archetypes ... 73
- The Object in the Dreamscape ... 75
- Three-Step Method ... 81

LUCID DREAMING ACTIVITIES ... 83

CHAPTER EIGHT: DREAM CHARACTERS AND ENCOUNTERS ... 84
- 12 Archetypes ... 90

CHAPTER NINE: EXPLORING YOUR DREAMSCAPE AND TOP 10 THINGS TO DO ... 96
- The Lay of the Land ... 96

CHAPTER TEN: WORKING WITH YOUR SPIRIT GUIDES ... 108
- Approaching Your Spirit Guides ... 110
- Connecting ... 113
- Inviting ... 115

CHAPTER ELEVEN: CREATING A DREAM SANCTUARY ... 118
- Shamanism's 3 Pillars ... 119
- The Role of the Dream Sanctuary ... 121

CHAPTER TWELVE: HEALING YOURSELF IN THE DREAMSCAPE 128
Promising Partners – Transpersonal Psychology 129
Definitions of Transpersonal Psychology, 1992 130
The OMNI Experiment 133

CHAPTER THIRTEEN: OVERCOMING NIGHTMARES AND SLEEP PARALYSIS 138
Nightmare Disorder 139
Imagery Rehearsal Therapy (IRT) 142
Sleep Paralysis in Lucid Dreaming 144
Reclaiming Control 145

CHAPTER FOURTEEN: WAKING UP (AND MAKING SENSE OF IT ALL) 148
Getting Grounded 148
Common Dream Symbols 150

CHAPTER FIFTEEN: CREATING LUCID ART AND WRITING 158
The Hidden Wellspring 159
Lucid Writing 159
Your Inner Rembrandt 162
Lucid Dreaming Is the Creator's Best Friend 163
Your Creative Journey 165

CHAPTER SIXTEEN: IMPROVE YOUR LIFE WITH LUCID DREAMING 167
Anxiety, Depression, and Psychosis 168
Motor Skill Rehabilitation – Learning New Skills 169
Equanimity and Emotional Control 171
Improved Problem-Solving and Enhanced Creativity 172
Improving the Life of Humanity with Lucid Dreaming 174

BONUS CHAPTER: LUCID DREAMING CHECKLIST 175
REFERENCES 180

Introduction

If you're reading this book, then you've probably experienced the phenomenon of lucid dreaming. You've been aware of your wakefulness while still dreaming. And you've wondered - how is that possible?

Until quite recently, it was believed that dreams only occurred while the brain was in the REM (rapid eye movement) section of the sleep cycle. But in 2016, researchers at Finland's Aalto University, in conjunction with colleagues at the University of Wisconsin, measured brain activity during the NREM (non-rapid eye movement) stage of sleep. They discovered that dreaming occurs in some people during this stage and that their brain activity resembles that of people who are awake. This research used a Transcranial Magnetic Stimulation With Electroencephalography (TMS-EEG) machine, capable of detecting changes in the neurophysiology of the brain.

The TMS-EEG has provided researchers in numerous studies with vital information about consciousness during sleep, under anesthesia, while awake, and in a state considered effectively vegetative. Research into how consciousness operates in all these physiological states opens the door to treating TBIs (traumatic brain injuries) in non-verbal patients. The TMS is already being used to treat illnesses like depression and short-circuit pain messages, reducing chronic and acute pain.

What all this means is that there is scientific support for lucid dreaming. That support began to accumulate starting in 1975, due to the work of Kenneth Hearne. Hearne is a parapsychologist who discovered that rapid eye movement occurred in those who experienced lucid dreams. While his findings were still constrained to the REM stage of the sleep cycle, he discovered that lucid dreaming always followed REM activity—the 2016 research sites lucid dreaming in NREM as well as REM or REM-adjacent sectors of the cycle.

So, here in the 21st Century, there's a small mountain of evidence that lucid dreaming is real and, what's more - that it's highly beneficial when you understand how to control it. And if you're an introspective person - someone who spends time with their thoughts, organizing and making sense of them - you're much more likely to have the ability to do that. You've probably already had lucid dreams. You're just not sure how to control them yet!

When you can control lucid dreams, you'll find:

- Anxiety is reduced. Lucid dreaming can impart a sense of empowerment and control. When you're dreaming in a state of awareness, you're in the driver's seat. You know how you want the dream to end, which can be enormously beneficial for those who deal with recurring nightmares, especially if they have PTSD (post-traumatic stress disorder), depression, substance abuse, or insomnia. Sleep paralysis may also be effectively addressed with using lucid dreaming.
- Better coordination. Lucid dreaming may be capable of improving your motor skills. When you visualize the motor skill you want to improve in a lucid dream, you activate the section of the brain responsible for making the movements,

enjoying the same effect as if you'd actually done the physical activity you're visualizing.

• Enhanced problem-solving. Researchers have also found evidence suggesting that lucid dreaming supports greater creativity in the process of solving problems, moving you beyond mere logic. Your creativity is generally improved through regular lucid dreaming.

• Improved sleep and overall wellness. When you're empowered, you're ready for what life throws at you. Having the ability to harness your consciousness is a tremendous advantage in life that rewards the practitioner with confidence and a more consistent sense of wellbeing.

I'm excited to share the concepts, techniques, and advice in this book with you, as I know that lucid dreaming can help so many people. Thank you for taking the time to read this book, and I hope you'll derive life-changing benefits from the information in it.

So, let's find out more and get down to the business of training our brains to dream lucidly!

Lucid Dreaming Essentials

Chapter One: The Science Behind Lucid Dreaming

"My notion would be, that anything which possesses any sort of power to affect another, or to be affected by another, if only for a single moment, however trifling the cause and however slight the effect, has real existence; and I hold that the definition of being is simply power."

Plato, Sophist dialog, 360 BCE

Empirical support for the claims I'm making in this book is abundant. So, in this chapter, I'd like to share some of the research and evidence arising, as I want you to feel comfortable with and confident about what you're going to read here.

You'll also be reading a bit about lucid dreaming in history and culture to provide a more holistic understanding of humanity's long-term relationship with it.

As I mentioned in the Introduction, research into lucid dreaming began in 1975 and was performed by a parapsychologist. But the most prominent voice in the study of lucid dreaming is undoubtedly Stephen LaBerge.

A *psychophysiologist* (concerned with the physiological foundation of psychology in the nerves and other bodily systems), LaBerge began studying the basis for his propositions about lucid dreaming while gaining his Ph.D. at Sanford University.

At the time, the idea of lucid dreaming was viewed with considerable suspicion. As we've discussed in the introduction, it was believed that dreaming of any kind took place only during rapid eye movement sleep. We now know this is only part of the story.

Throughout this book, we'll be visiting with Dr. LaBerge and reading about some techniques he used to train himself to dream lucidly. For now, we will talk about science and its gradual acceptance of lucid dreaming as a phenomenon of human consciousness.

What Is Consciousness?

Pinning down the nature of consciousness has been the grist of the philosophical and scientific mill for thousands of years.

The Greek philosopher, Plato, believed that consciousness was power – that for something to exist genuinely, it must impact the world around it. Plato simply described human consciousness as "being." Many were to follow Plato's concept of consciousness, driving it ever forward in philosophical exploration, from the 18th Century philosopher, Renee Descartes ("cogito ergo sum" or "I think; therefore I am") to the 20th Century's Jean-Paul Sartre (existentialism) and his contemporary, Maurice Merleau-Ponty (Phenomenology).

In 2008, the University of Wisconsin Madison's Center for Sleep and Consciousness's Giulio Tononi developed "integrated information theory," which is considered the most thorough explanation of consciousness to date. And what's striking about it is that, like Plato, neuroscientist Tononi's central thesis is that consciousness is an active agent, having the power of cause and effect on both the site of consciousness (that's you, my friends) and the world around it.

Melanie Boly, a neurologist at the University of Wisconsin's School of Medicine and Public Health, is a colleague of Tononi's, working to create a framework for testing the propositions of integrated information theory.

The sense is that the theory is correct, and the fact that it vindicates Plato's conception of consciousness is simply amazing. Through philosophical inquiry, this ancient philosopher pointed the way to the nature of consciousness - scientifically proven correct over 2,000 years later.

Integrated Information Theory

Theoretical physicist and mathematician at the Munich Center for Mathematical Philosophy in General Johannes Kleiner believe that the study of consciousness must be linked to the study of physics to illuminate our knowledge of how we perceive the world in the greater context of the universe and how it operates.

Working with Sean Tull, a University of Oxford mathematician, the philosophical underpinnings of the studies conducted to examine what consciousness is, from a mathematical and philosophical standpoint, based on what's known as "panpsychism." This area of philosophy posits that all matter is, to some degree, conscious, even to the smallest particle, implying a conscious universe.

But to create an empirical basis for the claim of universal consciousness in matter, Kleiner and Tull are in the process of developing a mathematical framework based on the human brain. What is the conscious experience of a computer? With the data derived from that information, a larger framework can be constructed and allied to other material realities - computers being only one.

Just ask Gerry Kasparov or Hal from 2001: A Space Odyssey! (Gerry Kasparov famously lost a chess game to a computer named "Big Blue," and Hal was a sentient computer in a space station that got a little full of himself).

While still a marginal area of scientific exploration, Panpsychism holds great promise for validating Tononi's integrated information theory by pinpointing the precise nature of consciousness and determining its reach and scope in the universe. And within the precise nature of consciousness is the tremendous power of lucid dreaming.

The Science of Lucid Dreaming

Published in May 2016, the study *Lucid Dreaming and the Big Five Personality Factors* found a strong correlation between these personality markers and the frequency with which people experienced lucid dreams.

For your reference, the five factors are:

- Extraversion
- Introversion
- Neuroticism
- Agreeableness
- Openness
- Conscientiousness

Those who modeled the personality trait "openness" were much more likely to have experienced lucid dreams, while those with the trait "agreeableness" were much less likely to have experienced them. Interestingly, those who modeled "neuroticism" (depression or anxiety) were also much more likely to experience lucid dreams.

The same study found that 51% of people had, at some point, had a lucid dreaming experience, while 20% of the study sample had lucid dreams regularly, at a rate of about one per month.

Another notable finding from the study revealed that children are much more likely to have regular lucid dreams, starting at about the age of 3. In adolescence, the frequency of lucid dreams begins to decline. Then, at the age of about 25, spontaneous lucid dreaming stops entirely.

The neurobiological basis for lucid or reflective/aware dreaming is murky. But a 2018 study discovered a connection between the frontopolar cortex and the temporoparietal association area. The study compared results gleaned from a group of people who experienced three lucid dreams per week and another, which experienced one lucid dream per year. But the study did not note any significant differences in the brain structure of the two groups.

What's of interest here is the anterior prefrontal cortex and its relationship to metacognitive functions ("thinking about thinking" or self-reflection).

Just this year, a study that involved interacting with lucid dreamers - as they were dreaming - was finally conducted. As Leonardo DiCaprio does in the film, Inception, researchers could communicate with people in their dream state for the first time.

Landmark Study on Lucid Dreaming

The study, implicating research teams from the Netherlands, Germany, France, and the United States, aimed to go further than past studies in establishing two-way communication between researchers and subjects.

This effort involved asking the dreamers questions that hadn't been posed in past training for the study. Implicated were 36 subjects. Of these, some were lucid dreamers with advanced experience, while others had not had a lucid dream in their lives but remembered at least one of the standard dreams they had each week. All participants were trained to recognize when they'd entered a dream state. Researchers explained lucid dreaming, then introduced simple cues fed to participants as they dreamed. These included specific sounds like fingers tapping. The cues would advise participants that they were dreaming.

Sleeping sessions were scheduled at various times – some took place at night and others in the early morning. Each of the four research teams involved employed a different means of communicating with dreamers. Some used flashing lights, while others used spoken questions. In addition, study participants were trained to signal researchers when they were dreaming. This involved prescribed cues, using the eyes and face.

Researchers tracked brain activity, facial muscle contractions, and eye movements as participants fell asleep. Participants were also fitted with ECG (electroencephalogram) helmets, fitted with electrodes.

Involving 57 unique sleep sessions, study results revealed that six participants signaled to researchers that they were experiencing lucid dreaming in 15 of 57 of the sessions. The participants were asked "yes" or "no" questions and simple math problems, responding with the pre-arranged signals researchers and participants had agreed upon. In the German research group, eye movements were guided by Morse code.

The four study groups combined posed 150 questions to the dreamers, with correct responses in 18.6% of the final sample, as reported in Current Biology. Only 3.2% of the questions were answered incorrectly, while 17.7% of responses were garbled and deemed indecipherable. In 60.8% of the sample, no response was made.

Researchers in the study concluded that the results indicated "proof of concept" (that, while results were somewhat inconclusive, they were on the right track). With the four labs involved employing varying communication tactics, the study proved that it was possible to communicate with people in a dream state.

After researchers had asked dreamers a series of questions, they were awakened and invited to describe the dreams they'd had. The results are interesting. In one case, a dreamer said that the math questions asked had been issued from a car radio. In another, the dreamer was at a party and heard the questions as though they were part of a movie narration. He recalled being asked if he spoke Spanish.

A cognitive neuroscientist at Northwestern University, Karen Konkoly, noted that the study indicated there's a better way to discover more about dreaming, generally, and lucid dreaming in particular. She believes that the techniques and strategies used in the study will prove valuable, therapeutically, for those who have experienced trauma. There are also hopeful applications for treating depression and anxiety.

While changing the course of people's dreams for psychological therapy or other purposes continues to reside solidly in the realm of science fiction, this study has opened the door to the possibility that our dreams can hold the key to lives unencumbered by the damage of trauma and other conditions. The study results indicate that applications may eventually manipulate creativity levels and improve problem-solving and skill development.

When the human mind enters the world of dreams, it enters the world of its subconscious, consisting of memories stored (but not necessarily remembered). With this new methodology for communicating with dreamers, the two-way communication model in the study may bring science-enhanced insights into that world of dreams, the playground of the subconscious.

Lucid Dreaming in History, Religion, and Philosophy

Lucid dreaming may have been part of the human experience in pre-history, but we'll stick to recorded history for our purposes.

Descriptions of lucid dreaming go back to at least 1,000 BCE, where we encounter the first recorded mention of it from in the Hindu Upanishads. There is even a name for lucid (or conscious) dreaming – "prajna." The word describes a state in which the dreamer has two simultaneously parallel realities in play. Conscious of inhabiting the dream state and their sleeping body simultaneously in prajna, both states are recognized by the person dreaming.

Prajna is the desired level of spiritual enlightenment in both Hinduism and Buddhism, both actively sought after in the practice of Yoga Nidra (known as "dream Yoga" in the West). Yoga nidra, recognized by Tibetan Buddhism among other Asian philosophical movements, has popularized lucid dreaming as a spiritual pursuit all over Asia, where lucid dreaming has been recognized for over 30 centuries.

While the influence of Indian spiritual practices began to be disseminated in Tibet, the Bonpo tradition utilized lucid dreaming as a spiritual tool for over 12,000 years, according to practitioners. Bonpo is an animistic, indigenous tradition and the homegrown precursor to Tibetan Buddhism.

In the West, Aristotle was the first to describe lucid dreaming in the book, On Dreams (350 BCE), specifically, "...when one is asleep, there is something in consciousness which tells us that what presents itself is but a dream".

Centuries later, in 415 CE, St. Augustine recorded the observations recounted to him from lucid dreams experienced by Gennadius, a physician in Carthage (Augustine's Letter to the priest, Evodius). Two dreams are referred to, in which Gennadius describes the appearance of a youth who appears in them. The two discuss Gennadius's state of consciousness (whether he's dreaming or awake).

In the second dream, the youth asks Gennadius if he recognizes him and, if so, from where. Gennadius says that he does. The young man tells Gennadius that the previous dream is where the two know each other from. They conclude that Gennadius is experiencing simultaneous consciousness and the dream state - or lucid dreaming. The fullness of the tale is that Gennadius was having doubts about the afterlife. The two-part lucid dream validated the existence of an afterlife, thus allaying Gennadius's doubts on the matter.

Lucid dreaming has a significant presence in historical Islam, especially among mystics of the Faith.

Lailat al-Miraj describes one of the key events in the life of the Prophet Mohammed (570 - 632 CE) and one of the most important dates on the Islamic calendar. A two-part spiritual and physical journey, Lailat al-Miraj describes two distinct events which take place on the same night:

- **The Isra** - The first part of the journey sees the Prophet riding a winged horse to a far-flung place of prayer, where he prays with other prophets.
- **The Mi-raj** - On the second part of the journey, the Prophet ascends to the Divine, where God tells Mohammed the esoteric details of prayers, instructing the Prophet to take these back to the people.

Described in the Qu'ran (sura Al-Isra) and in greater detail in the Hadith, the parallels to lucid dreaming are clear. Somewhat parallel to the vision of the chariot in the Biblical Book of Ezekiel, the Lailat al-Miraj describes an experience somewhere between waking reality and dreaming. In the experience of the Prophet are the seeds of Islam's mystics, especially the Sufi. But other Muslim thinkers were to recount similar experiences.

Ibn El-Arabi, a 12th Century Sufi, believed that the ability to control consciousness in dreams and drive the action was a type of litmus test for mystics, suggesting lucid dreaming as a rite of passage those aspiring to that status.

In the 15th Century, Persian Sufi mystic Shamsoddin Lahiji recounted a vision arising during his meditations. In it, he "saw the entire universe, in the structure it presents, consists of light."

While there is no way for us to verify these were lucid dreams in the way we think of them, visions and their cultural significance are unmistakably a tremendous feature of all three monotheistic Near Eastern religions. This is seen in Hebrew Scripture in visions of bones dancing, mysterious, terrifying theophanies, and chariots with thousands of eyes. In Christianity, we see an example in the description of Jesus's 40 days in the desert. But throughout the long histories of all three major monotheistic Faiths, the tradition of dreams and visions is continued among the ranks of the mystics of the Jewish, Christian, and Islamic Faiths.

Despite the impediment of varying levels of cultural significance as to what differentiates dreams from visions and whether any such differentiation exists, the common, human thread is clear. From the East to the West, recorded history has provided us with many instances of chronicled dreams, which seem to resemble the content and tone of lucid dreams. Such dreams in disconnected global cultures point to a fundamental truth about lucid dreaming; it's both a relatively common human experience and one that serves a distinct spiritual purpose.

Cultural Impact

According to a study entitled, Lucid dreaming: Effects of culture in a US American sample (Schredl, M. & Bulkley, K, 2020), material differences exist between predominately individualistic cultures and those that adhere to a communal sociocultural model.

The study found these cultural differences were very strong in their sample of 3,992 participants aged 18 and over. An overall instance of those in the sample experiencing lucid dreaming was 35.72%.

A sharp difference was revealed between Latino participants and those of European background, with European-Americans (Caucasians) experiencing a higher frequency of lucid dreams. The reason for this disparity is believed to be the individualistic/communal contrast of the two cultural frameworks in play, with Caucasians being more individualistic and Latinos more communal.

But the study concludes that this distinction requires more study to apply the presenting suggestion about culture to a broader sample of participants.

As we've discussed above, lucid dreaming has a long and illustrious history in Western religious contexts. But in Christianity, since the advent of the Roman Empire and the ascension of Christianity to the position of Imperial religion, dreaming has been viewed by the Church with suspicion and even, at times, hostility. For example, Thomas Aquinas (1225 - 1274) believed there were four specific types of dreams, with the 4th being produced either by God, demons, or other spiritual presences.

Aquinas's attitude toward the role of dreams in spirituality was not entirely hostile. He did, however, believe that prophetic dreams were most probably demonic deceptions.

It wasn't until the 17th Century that lucid dreaming peeked out of its exile in the West, finding an embrace in the European Enlightenment. During this era, popular philosophy became focused on discovering the inner life of the rational human mind.

Rene Descartes (1596 – 1650) was a fervent believer in lucid dreaming, keeping a record of his own experiences of it in a 12-page manuscript never published and eventually lost. However, his thinking on these dreams influenced his work. This document was to become what is known as the *Olympica.*

Unknown until the publication of Descartes' biography (1691), the Olympica detailed three dreams experienced by the philosopher on the night of November 10, 1619. What Descartes was reported to have experienced, as a 23-year-old man, was to change the course of philosophical history.

In the first of these dreams, the sleeping Descartes senses weakness on his right side, so he rolls onto his left, which prompts the second dream to begin (dream state + physical awareness=lucid dreaming). Similarly, when Descartes awakens due to a loud, crashing sound in the second dream, he witnesses lights twinkling in the darkness of his room.

The third dream is quite detailed. Descartes feels a book in his hand and is compelled to turn to something in it. He does so and reads the question, "What path of life shall I pursue?" Descartes attached tremendous meaning to this series of lucid dreams and would henceforth maintain that they were why he took the path in life he did.

While lucid dreaming has a long, global history and empirical, scientific support for its existence, there are still misconceptions. So, our next job will be to clear some of those up.

Chapter Two: Common Misconceptions about Lucid Dreaming

"People think you're crazy if you talk about things they don't understand."

Elvis Presley

Understanding is what makes the world go around. If we all understood each other and the world around us as well as we should, it could readily be argued that the world would be a more peaceful place.

And part of the problem with lucid dreaming's public profile, even today, is that it is misunderstood. It's often confused with astral projection (or other types of out-of-body experiences), for example, or with shamanic journeying.

We'll contrast those states of consciousness against lucid dreaming shortly. But because we're talking about misconceptions, perhaps we should take a moment to acknowledge the distorted view the media sometimes takes toward concepts that challenge traditional ideas of consciousness. The case of Jared Loughner is a rather poignant instance of this.

On January 8, 2011, Jared Loughner killed six people, injuring 14 others outside a Tucson, Arizona Safeway. Among the injured was U.S. Representative Gabby Giffords, now renowned for her courage in recovery from the serious wounds she sustained.

Obsessed with movies like Matrix and Inception, Loughner had a fixation on lucid dreaming. An undiagnosed schizophrenic, Loughner had been pushed out of his community college. Several fellow students were reportedly uncomfortable in his presence.

In a series of YouTube videos, Loughner appeared to be confusing reality with the dreamscape that heavily influenced him. As a person with schizophrenia, Loughner's apprehension of reality was already challenged by his mental health condition. It's quite possible that the idea of lucid dreaming promised an understandable framework for a disorder of the mind he didn't understand.

News organizations across the country ran with the lucid dreaming theme, running headlines asking if Loughner had thought he was dreaming when he committed the atrocity in Tucson.

The Loughner story bled, and for as long as more lugubrious interest could be added, it *led*. This is an old story in popular information. Satanic cults murdering children sold more newspapers and advertising space than shadowy lone killers. Being depicted as believing himself to be dreaming while committing a crime, Jared Loughner fits the same description by fulfilling the same purpose.

But the Loughner example is not the only one. Hollywood has sensationalized lucid dreaming, which is not entirely its fault. While the film industry isn't necessarily responsible for literal interpretations of fictional content, it's clear there's a problem with public interpretation verging on the fantastical. The reification (making an abstract, theoretical construct sound as if it is concrete truth) of the "Illuminati" in The Da Vinci Code is a good example. A line is crossed in the imagination, and suddenly, a young man with schizophrenia is shooting innocent people – "because he's dreaming."

Orson Welles's <u>War of the Worlds</u>, when broadcast over the radio in 1938, caused mass panic among listeners. The line between fantasy and reality had been crossed, prompting an unhinged public response. That line is even more easily crossed when the listener suffers from a mental health condition that distorts reality.

Associating lucid dreaming with the reality of the material world is problematic and indicative of psychological disturbance. This is the point proven by Loughner's obsession with lucid dreaming. Having found an organizing framework for his disordered thinking, Loughner believed that his "dream" actions were inconsequential as they weren't occurring in the material world but in the dreamscape.

The Loughner story is just one example of how hype and misrepresentation can sometimes meld into a soup of public credulity, and, unfortunately, lucid dreaming has been a victim of that effect. One reason I wanted to write this book is to contribute to the growing body of positive evidence of the reality, and enormous benefit to humanity, of lucid dreaming. Adding to a positive narrative is how enduring influence on the public consciousness is exerted.

But to appreciate the positive, knowing about prevailing misconceptions provides a more holistic view of the subject. When we understand the misunderstanding, we can deconstruct and correct it!

Let's look at some common misconceptions in popular culture about lucid dreaming.

Shared Lucid Dreams

In the film, Inception, characters share their lucid dreaming events simultaneously as they're dreaming.

Sorry, friends. This simply does not happen. So if you were planning a lucid dreaming Zoom as a team-building exercise at work, cross that off your list right now.

Explaining meshing dreams, these are two dreams that are not "shared" but contain coincidental elements.

Getting Stuck in a Dream

Here, we have another myth generated by the film, Inception. In the film, powerful pharmaceuticals assist participants on their journey to the lucid dream space, which is not recommended for this book's purposes!

There is no truth to the idea that you can be stuck inside your dreams. Most dreams take no more than 20 minutes to play out and many, much less time. But you are never stuck, especially when you have the right techniques at your disposal to awaken yourself. Even people who experience only conventional dreams have access to this ability. The trick is simply to think about the fact that you dream, reflect on it and understand it as part of your psychological makeup. Once you are in conversation with the fact that you dream, you are empowered to decide when you wake up.

After reading this book, you'll understand that dreamers can awaken themselves even in conventional dreams. The only exception to this is sleep paralysis, which is unrelated to the speculative fictional narrative in Inception and which we'll discuss in more detail later on in this volume.

Lucid Dreaming is Evidence of Mental Illness

As presented above, news media around the mass shooting in Tucson was sensationalized by discovering that the perpetrator was obsessed with lucid dreaming. But Loughner unwittingly drew an intellectual parallel between lucid dreaming and his own mental health challenges. Lucid dreaming provided a template to rationalize his thinking, not as disordered, but as that of a master of the art of lucid dreaming.

But it was a mental illness that led to Loughner's obsession, not lucid dreaming, that led to mental illness. Nor was lucid dreaming, itself, proof that Loughner was ill. Rather, it provided a disordered young man with a template for interfacing with the chaotic nature of his own relationship to material reality. It provided him with an explanation.

Lucid Dreaming Is Wishful Thinking

As we've discussed earlier in this book, lucid dreaming has been scientifically studied since 1975, with new information arising as recently as 2021. With each new study, more is known about the biopsychological underpinnings of lucid dreaming.

Lucid dreaming has been with humanity for its conscious history, as you've read. But only now are we learning the fullness of the truth. Only in the 20th Century did we begin to amass evidence that proves its existence and science is never about wishful thinking.

Only the "Spiritual" Have Lucid Dreams

While the spiritually aware have lucid dreams, so do children. Children have little awareness of the spiritual constructs of adulthood. They have simple ideas about God being love and the world around them being good. They are unbound by adult constructs, allowing their creativity to take flight.

Earlier in this book, I told you that 55% of people had experienced lucid dreaming. They're not all children, either. Many adults have lucid dreams. Some of them only have several over the course of their lives. Others may have them several times per week. But only a handful of this group employs a set of techniques to engage with their dream lives this way. Certainly, children don't!

Many people interested in harnessing the power of lucid dreaming do so to enhance their lives. They may or may not be of a spiritual disposition.

Lucid dreaming harms your mental health

While this statement is largely incorrect, discernment, caution, and moderation are useful guides in all things. A couple of items here should be garner our attention, according to an article by Dr. Nirit Soffer-Dudek of Ben Gurion University, in Israel. Her comments regarding the potential impact of lucid dreaming on well-being are worth noting, as she is a leading researcher in the field.

Soffer-Dudek points out two areas of potential vulnerability:

- Sleep quality/disruption
- Potential for blurring the boundary between fantasy and reality (keeping in mind, as you read, the example of Jared Loughner, challenged by schizophrenia).

We've discussed the dangers of popularization in media and entertainment – namely, that ideas can be distorted through the repetition of fallacious or incomplete information. We can take away from Soffer-Dudek's warning that lucid dreaming is a verifiable state of consciousness that must be taken seriously. Lucid dreaming, as discussed earlier, can set the stage for a variety of life improvements. What lucid dream is not is an amusement park or a substitute for waking material reality.

Lucid dreaming is a helper, not a servant, and perhaps when we fail to understand that, we do ourselves and the growing lucid dreaming community harm.

There is no evidence to suggest that lucid dreaming is harmful to mental health beyond the potential to perhaps exacerbate existing mental health conditions. As I've pointed out in the case of Jared

Loughner, lucid dreaming provided a framework for the schizophrenia that provoked Loughner's tenuous grasp of reality. It did not create the mental health condition already in play.

That said, to prove itself, lucid dreaming must be more rigorously examined to allay any suspicion it may contribute to mental health vulnerabilities or poor or disrupted sleep quality, according to Soffer-Dudek.

Lucid Dreaming Heals Physical Illnesses and Maladies

Just as lucid dreaming is not your servant, lucid dreaming is not your snake-wielding faith healer.

Lucid dreaming can and often does support the healing of mental health conditions, blockages in our intellectual and spiritual well-being, and the scars of the past. But if you're hoping it will heal a broken bone or a tumor, I'm sorry to report that lucid dreaming doesn't work that way.

However, the well-being that most often accompanies the practice of lucid dreaming will certainly support your journey as you navigate serious physical health conditions and realities more successively.

Popular media can dramatically affect the way people look at the world, and lucid dreaming hasn't been spared. The public's acceptance of popular media claims sometimes crosses the reality-fantasy barrier in a strange transfiguration of fiction to fact. This is the case with the reification of fantasy arising from films like Inception. While not intended to be factual, misconceptions arising from the film's plot persist. Hopefully, we've dispelled some here.

As promised earlier, I'd like to turn to some of the prevailing confusion around alternative states of consciousness. It's important to understand lucid dreaming as a separate phenomenon from shamanic journeying or OBEs (out-of-body experiences). However, there are connections between the three states. Existing autonomously, they're also linked, to a degree, as part of a psychobiological framework.

Let's examine these states of consciousness separately, then turn to how they're interrelated.

Out of Body Experience

Our bodies, the French phenomenologist Maurice Merleau-Ponty wrote, are the human way of having a world. His understanding of the body's role in consciousness was a reference point from which we know the world and the world knows us.

An OBE describes an experience during which we feel disconnected from the body. Sometimes, those who experience them describe looking on down on themselves from a height. Others describe floating outside their bodies. The sense is that the person experiencing an OBE is dissociated from the body. While this is occurring, the sensation is every bit as real as waking up in the morning.

Neurological conditions like epilepsy and migraines may be responsible for some OBEs and stress and anxiety, but 10% of people have experienced one in their lifetime. OBEs occur without warning and are generally short-lived.

A 2004 study authored by Olaf Blanke examined the neural (nervous system) basis for OBEs, concluding that they're linked to the brain's cognitive processing function. Blanke believes this area of study may reveal valuable information about our self-conceptions as a whole, as human organisms. How does our mind inhabit our body but seem able to transcend it simultaneously? This is a question that's seldom considered but part and parcel of the mind/body dichotomy in religious and philosophical discourse. Blanke's work promises to find a way forward with this enduring philosophical exploration.

Shamanic Journeying

Shamanism originated in pre-history among hunter-gatherer societies. The Shaman's role was to interact with the Deity and intercede on behalf of the people he represented, using a trance state to seek healing, answers to questions, accompany the dead to the underworld, and guide the people, and even to make rain. Shamanism is the locus classicus of institutionalized religion, bearing many of its hallmarks, including belief in a higher power, concurrent with the belief that the higher power would punish unorthodoxy (wrong thinking) as defined by the Shaman's understanding.

Shamanic journeying was the practice of the Shaman and those he directed in this practice. Entering a trance state, the inverted spirit world (underworld) could be entered. The Shaman or those he led would return from the trance journey with what was sought when they embarked on it.

Today, the concept of Shamanic journeying has entered the lexicon of psychology, becoming a healing tool in therapists' hands and providing a useful therapeutic self-help framework to those seeking healing. That such an ancient practice should be used in this innovative way is rather amazing. Stripped of its religious trappings, Shamanic journeying has provided many patients with psychological challenges a potent tool.

In a purely modern, secular sense, the Shamanic journey takes one within – to the inverted spirit world of hunter-gathering Shamans that might just as well represent the subconscious – self-interrogating the hidden parts of yourself, in that world.

Of the three states of consciousness we're discussing, the Shamanic journey features the strongest religious component in its original form. Today, though, it has found a practical application for people of all beliefs or no belief at all. The Shamanic journey has been personalized toward producing sounder mental health in those who practice it therapeutically. The Shamanic journey has evolved from a communal expression of spiritual leadership to become a transformative personal journey.

But the tradition of Shamanism lives on around the world, the journey maintaining its original meaning.

Astral Projection

Astral projection is the state of consciousness that lucid dreaming is most often confused with, even though the two are fundamentally different.

Astral projection posits reaching out with the soul/mind/perception in an intentional way. This personal aspect of consciousness then ascends or travels to a premeditated objective. This is the core difference between astral projection and lucid dreaming and astral projection and OBEs. There is no projection of consciousness outward in lucid dreaming, and OBEs are sudden and unforeseen.

Projecting to an insubstantial plane is a journey of consciousness seeking answers. But it's what's presumed to be projected which is of interest. This is an "astral body," differentiated from the physical body of the projector. The belief is this astral body has its own cognitive function – a separate consciousness.

There is no evidence for astral projection, even though it has existed in various forms as a narrative device in various world religions for thousands of years of human history. That a separate, immaterial body can somehow function independently of the physical body is akin to belief in the soul – similarly unproven by empirical inquiry.

As you have seen, any comparison between lucid dreaming and any state of consciousness (alleged and otherwise) we've walked through above is inaccurate. Lucid dreaming isn't a device to transport you to an unknown, spiritual plane. It's not a journey to the underworld or a sudden dissociation with your body in its real-world place. Lucid dreaming is a means of working with your dream state to learn, grow and become a more fully realized person.

Neither servant nor faith healer, lucid dreaming is a way to enjoy a renewed relationship with your mind's hidden depths. Let's discover more in Chapter 3, where we'll talk about getting you prepared to dream lucidly.

Chapter Three: Getting Prepared for Lucid Dreaming

"The will to succeed is important, but what's more important is the will to prepare."

Bobby Knight

Preparing yourself for lucid dreaming is an essential component to successfully experiencing the power of this state of consciousness.

As with anything in life worth doing that you've never done before, preparation is what focuses your mind on understanding your own mental landscape in the dream space and directing it toward the consciousness you desire to be alive to in your dreams. Your will to succeed at experiencing lucid dreaming is already there. Now, you need to align that will with your will to prepare. As the quote at the beginning of this chapter counsels, the will to prepare is the essential piece of the puzzle.

This chapter will discuss what you need to do to ensure your success in achieving the lucid dreaming state of consciousness. What I'm offering readers here is not a series of technical descriptions. Rather, I will share with you what I've learned from my own experiences of lucid dreaming and the role that certain practices played in preparing me for them.

Preparation is a process, and to this process, be prepared to dedicate a week to arrive at the point at which you feel confident to proceed with lucid dreaming. Schedule the week when you're ready to start, ensuring that you have the time to dedicate to your preparations. Clear your calendar. Give yourself the time and space you need to commit yourself to the preparation required.

Gather All Relevant Information

You're reading this book, which means you've already started your preparations. While it provides the basics you'll need to get started with lucid dreaming, this book is just the tip of the information iceberg.

Don't Stop Here!

Instead, expand your understanding of lucid dreaming by following the links in the section at the end of this book entitled "Resources." Go down the rabbit hole prepared to learn. Read everything you can get your hands on. But remember – not all information on the Internet is reliable. While I shouldn't need to tell you that, you must be able to distinguish between quality information and "other" information. Remember that peer-reviewed studies are your best bet, along with writing and interviews with those who write and participate in such studies.

Another excellent source of information is dreamers themselves. Seek those who will chat with you about their experiences of lucid dreaming. (I've included links to quality contact points in the resources.) Join one or all the groups listed and chat with others who share your interest in lucid dreaming. Remember to test information against what you've learned in this book and elsewhere from those implicated in research into lucid dreaming.

The three online groups I've included are on diverse platforms (Facebook, Reddit, and a website dedicated to lucid dreaming). Your awareness of the truth about lucid dreaming will help you navigate some of the more colorful commentaries you're likely to find on Reddit. Dive in, engaging your critical thinking capacity as you do!

Don't forget to raise the topic with your circle. You may discover that others you know are exploring lucid dreaming. And it doesn't get better than that. Honest, open discussions with people you know and trust provide a great medium for learning and sharing information with others.

Sifting through the information helps focus your mind on where you want to go and how you mean to get there. Knowledge is powerful. Just remember that quality information is the definition of knowledge.

Dream Journaling

I'm a huge fan of all kinds of journaling. Writing down our thoughts and experiences is a method of self-examination leading to self-knowledge. It's a discipline that can reap incredible rewards for several purposes.

But for this book, keeping a journal detailing your dreams allows you to survey the kinds of symbols you're experiencing in your conventional dreams. Examining these is like having a tiny probe into your subconscious. Symbols in your dreams stand in for daylight problem-solving, pointing out aspects of various life circumstances that your conscious mind may have missed. The subconscious has its own interpretational framework, unavailable to us when we're awake, for the most part.

Your dream journal should be kept next to your bed so that no matter what time you wake up – in the middle of the night, following a particularly intense dream or first thing in the morning - it's there, ready for you to record your dreams.

Next to your dream journal, there should be a functioning pen. Check that ready to write, as there's nothing worse than waking from a dream you're itching to record to find that your pen is dry or missing!

Writing isn't the only way to record your dreams. Some like to sketch what they dream. Others produce more elaborate imagery to record the flavor and colors of what they've encountered in the dream space. Some people even prefer to record their dreams on a voice recording device, as they find their own handwriting illegible. I'm sure many of you can relate to the fact that handwriting may be somewhat impaired when opening your eyes from a night's sleep, so this option may work best for you.

Should you choose to write your dream journal, you'll be interested to know there are journals on the market specifically designed for people to record their dreams. These provide specific tools, like grids and related prompts that provide you with a structure for recording your dreams.

Regardless of the method you choose for creating a dream record, you'll also need a dream *dictionary* to look up the symbols revealed to you in your dreams. These can be very handy when certain items (spiders, dogs with oddly hued fur, celebrities, landmarks you've never seen, among many other symbols) appear in your dreams.

So, how does recording the content of your dreams assist you with the goal of lucid dreaming? Let's review:

- **Patterns Revealed**

Consistently maintaining a record of your dreams can reveal patterns in the dreams you have. Recurring dreams, for example, can be the same each time or feature key details which evolve.

You may also notice certain presences in your dreams which repeatedly appear, even when the dream differs from others you've had. These can be people you know, animals, or places.

- **Creativity Released**

Creative people often complain of being "blocked." No matter how creative you are, most creative people have moments in their lives when the creative juices just aren't flowing. Keeping a dream journal can help with that. Your subconscious is always working on the problems your conscious mind can't seem to solve. By journaling about your dreams, you have a window into the secret solutions being worked out in your subconscious.

- **Mind Prepared for Lucid Dreaming**

Documenting your dreams is also part of preparing for lucid dreaming. Keep a journal of your dreams habituates your conscious mind to the work of the subconscious in dreams. As you become more familiar with your dreams and recognize patterns, familiar subjects, and symbols, you'll begin to understand how your mind works while you sleep and how it helps you resolve conditions in waking life.

I find that when I write things down, I don't forget them. I also tend to think more deeply about whatever I've written. There's something about the act of writing which concretizes your thoughts. The interaction between your brain and your hand as it writes creates a profound integration of thought/dream in the physical action of writing. Even if I'm writing nothing more profound than a grocery list, I remember what I've written to the point I often no longer need to look at the list.

Some Tips for Dream Journaling

- The moment you wake up, you should be reaching for a journal to record the dream or dreams you've had while sleeping. If you can catch the images and scenarios while they're still fresh in your mind, you'll be able to capture more detail.
- Write about your dreams in the present tense, as though they were happening at the moment. The sense of immediacy this will lend your journaling can spur greater recall and resurrect details you may not have been aware of when you first woke up. Placing yourself in action in "real-time" instigates a higher rate of recall.
- Emotions are key to dream journaling. How you felt in the dream is an indicator of the message. Were you happy? Frightened? Confused? These emotions point to the dream's message to you. What was the context? Were you in a familiar place or one unknown to you? How did the context of the dream make you feel?

Preparing Your Physical Space

The room you sleep in should be treated as a sacred space. Your attention to detail here matters because this is the space in which you dream. If dreaming is important to you and you're here to make a serious attempt at lucid dreaming, then you'll understand what I mean.

Too often, the place we sleep at night is an afterthought. We leave our beds unmade. We read or surf the internet in bed or watch television. Once a sanctuary of peace, the bedroom has become more of an all-purpose crash zone, and that's not conducive to the work of learning lucid dreaming techniques.

So, let's talk about how to make your bedroom the sacred space you need it to be to enable lucid dreaming.

Light

Taking care of light in your bedroom is a good practice, even if you're not interested in lucid dreaming. Streetlights and porch lights, and lights from commercial installations, like stores and shopping malls, can invade your space. Investing in a set of blackout curtains is a practical way to keep your room dark enough for sleep.

But ambient light isn't the only enemy of lucid dreaming. Blue light from electronics is another problem. This type of light is emitted by cellular devices, Kindles, laptops, and any kind of device with a screen. Even a television in the bedroom should be banished as it is a blue light source. So, if you're the person who likes to lie in bed and scroll through social media, maybe it is better to do that on the couch from now on.

But why? What's wrong with blue light? It blocks melatonin, the hormone produced by your body to make you drowsy. You're in your room to sleep, and blue light can make it difficult or even impossible to fall asleep and stay asleep, so keep it out of your sleep space.

Sound

We all have those nights when our deep sleep is interrupted by outside noise. That could be wailing sirens, yowling cats, barking dogs, or the neighbors having a loud spat. Whatever it is, you don't need it!

There are several things you can do to maintain a quiet sleeping space. One is the blackout curtains mentioned earlier. These are heavy enough to dampen the sound coming from outside.

Your cellular phone should be turned off when you sleep. Most events in life aren't that important, and if someone wants to wake you up, they can always show up to bang on your front door.

If noise regularly disturbs your sleep, a set of quality earplugs can be helpful. Also, think about investing in a pair of noise-canceling earphones. These block external noise, but you can add to the effect by listening to "white noise" tapes. Ocean sounds, the wind rustling leaves, ambient music – all these are great alternatives for adding peaceful sounds to your sleep space that keep out the wailing, yowling, and yelling of a noisy world.

If you live with other people, your sleep must be respected. If your housemates are given to being loud after hours, that's a problem crying out for a solution, so solve it. Talk to them about how important sleep is to you. Hang a "do not disturb" sign on your door at night. In the worst-case scenario, find more respectful housemates. If we're talking about your family, then it's time to train them!

Training Your Brain

One of the most important undertakings in the project of preparing yourself for lucid dreaming is training your brain.

Training your brain for lucid dreaming addresses changes that occur while in this state of consciousness. For example, during normal dreams, the frontotemporal cortex is not "free" to operate in the same way as it does during lucid dreaming. In a lucid dream, this part of the brain is much more engaged. Gamma waves also increase in this state, causing neurons to fire at a rate comparable to that present in waking consciousness. The same effect occurs when we use our brain for "executive functions," like decision-making and our voluntary actions.

Let's review some training tools that you may use at your discretion in your preparations.

Binaural Beats

Binaural beats are really a trick your brain plays on you. When you listen to a soundscape in which two tones are juxtaposed at varying frequencies, you hear a binaural beat. Take a moment to do a quick search for binaural beats on YouTube to experience the sound I'm describing.

Located in the brain stem, the superior olivary complex is the brain's "first mover" in the processing and interpretation of sound. Hearing sounds set at different frequencies, your brain interprets and experiences the sound like a "beat." when it encounters binaural beats, brain waves shift, and the activity of neurons is synchronized (entrainment). This synchronization process in neuronal activity produces the ability to attain the state of consciousness used in lucid dreaming.

Specifically, in the case of deploying binaural beats to train your brain for lucid dreaming, you'll want to address the theta and delta brain waves.

- **Theta:** These brainwaves govern the brain in the transition from wakefulness to sleep just before you sleep. This is the threshold of consciousness, in which you're still awake but on your way to sleep and very relaxed.
- **Delta:** Delta brainwaves govern the deep sleep the human brain experiences after each 90-minute sleep cycle. Delta transforms the experiences we have each day into long-term memories. This function allows us to make meaning from our daily lives.

For our purposes, I recommend addressing the Theta brainwaves, as these represent the precise state of consciousness we're shooting for with lucid dreaming.

There is no conclusive scientific support for binaural beats and their efficacy. However, there is some evidence that binaural beats support better focus, relaxation, and memory. A study undertook in 2017 rendered results that suggest that higher frequency binaural beats correlate with enhanced attention (see link in References).

I recommend you take no less than 30 minutes per day to listen to binaural beats. This is considered the threshold for training, where you want to get your brain to prepare for your lucid dreaming adventure. Remember those noise-canceling headphones we talked about earlier in this chapter? Here's another use for them!

Meditation

Meditation is not necessarily a difficult discipline. Its applications and techniques vary wildly in a world hungry for peace and the sensation of feeling centered in a world that's increasingly a blur of fast-paced technology, imagery, and information.

Meditation is for everyone. It's accessible and not at all difficult to accustom yourself to as you add it to your life.

Here are simple tips to get you started.

- Block off enough time to ensure you're relaxed and unrushed. Meditation is not something you "squeeze in." It's something you hive off time for. Give yourself an hour to set the scene and to ensure you're relaxed. You may lay down or sit comfortably on a chair or a cushion or yoga mat on the floor.
- Choose a time of day during which you won't be interrupted. Early morning and late in the evening before bed is perfect times for meditation.
- Start by intentionally inhaling and exhaling slowly. As you do so, imagine that you're expelling tension with each exhalation, breathing in pure relaxation and calm. Allow your mind to wander where it will. You'll encounter fleeting thoughts. Ignore them. You may note them as you would someone passing on the street you don't know. Focus on your slow inhalations and exhalations.
- Once you feel relaxed, note your inner monologue, and then ignore it as you relax the muscles of your body. At this point, you can visualize (more on that below).

Don't be distressed by your mind wandering as you seek a meditative state (which is relaxed and aware without attending to the minutiae that commonly plagues the human mind). Simply allow your thoughts to occur without judging them in any way. Allow them to pass you by.

Visualization

A key part of your meditation should be visualizing yourself in a natural setting. This involves noting sensory details like scent, sound, touch, and taste. If you're next to a lake, you may smell plants growing nearby or the scent of grilling hamburgers from a nearby campsite. You may hear birds or the wind rustling the leaves in the trees you're surrounded by. You may taste the tang of the BBQ smoke from the hamburgers. Do you feel hungry? (Remembering that your emotional landscape is the most important of all when entering the lucid dreamscape).

Visualizing yourself in a natural setting while being keenly aware of the experience runs parallel to the eventual act of lucid dreaming itself. The more detailed you are in the visualization, the more in tune your brain is with the imagined experience. If you're using binaural beats, this process will begin to come easily to you, as your brain is being trained on several fronts – that of the soundscape, meditation, and the visualization accompanying your meditative time.

Now that you have some crucial tools at your disposal to prepare your brain for its lucid dreaming adventure, we're ready to enter the next phase of your development as a lucid dreamer.

In the next section are several chapters describing what you'll experience. You'll discover what to expect, and the elements of entering lucidity and controlling the dreamscape.

Get ready to learn how to get to the land of lucidity and what to do there!

Start Lucid Dreaming

Chapter Four: Basic Induction Techniques

Lucid dreaming has been extensively studied, but there is still much about it that's unknown. One aspect of the discussion which is abundantly clear, however, is that of induction techniques.

We know that these techniques are successful, as they've been employed in the studies I've just mentioned by researchers. To study lucid dreaming, you need a lucid dreamer, and so techniques that induce this state of consciousness have been an essential component of moving toward greater clarity in the research community's understanding.

There are several key induction techniques I'd like to share with you in this chapter. The most important thing to remember as we move into the stage of inducing lucid dreaming is that everyone is different. Some of us dream lucidly more easily than others, and for some, one technique will be more effective than others. But as you're just getting started, I strongly suggest that you try all the techniques discussed in this chapter to see how they work and, more importantly, how they work for you. Combining these techniques was found to be the most reliable method in the 2017 Australian lucid dream induction study. So, learn, test, and work on finding the induction technique or combination of techniques that are your "perfect fit."

So, let's dive in and discover how to induce the lucid dreaming state of consciousness.

Reality Testing

Metacognition is when you think about thinking. This is our analytical mind asking itself questions about the way it thinks and learns. Reality testing trains your mind to notice its awareness and to analyze, test, or check in on it.

Checking in on your state of consciousness is an act of self-consciousness that examines where your mind is at. Are you dreaming? Are you awake?

But there's more to reality testing than asking yourself if you're awake. Awareness of the environment you're asking the question in is also key to this technique's effectiveness. Further, your relationship with that environment and how you're navigating it informs the question by feeding back to your mind the "realness" of your consciousness. Confirming what that consists of means using your senses and making a mental note of what they're telling your brain.

Reality testing should be conducted throughout the day, at intervals of 2 or 3 hours. If you think you'll have difficulty remembering to do your reality tests, you may wish to set the alarm on your computer or phone.

Your senses are really the key to effective reality testing. This induction technique is highly effective when you choose only one of the real tests listed below. Choose one of these and then stick to it. Repetition of the words "Am I awake?" is the verbal cue that accompanies the test you choose.

Looking in a Mirror

Because of the mobile nature of our lives, you may find you need to use mirrors at different locations. That's not a problem. Any mirror will do.

Look into the mirror and ask the question, "Am I awake?" Then look at yourself. Is that your face? Do you appear the same to yourself as you normally do when you look at yourself in the mirror? Are those the clothes you put on in the morning?

Looking at a Part of Your Body

Any part of your body will do but if you're going to use this reality test, choose only one, like your hands or feet. As I said above, keeping this item consistent will assist in induction.

So, look at your hands, feet, knees, or whatever else you can see. Does everything look the way it normally does? Have you grown an extra finger or two? Do you have three legs? Choose the visible body part you will use as a test.

Test Your Breathing

With your mouth closed, pinch your nostrils together? If you can't breathe, you're awake. If you can, you're dreaming!

Check the Time

As you ask yourself, "Am I awake?" look at the time. Look away and then look back. Has the time changed in the nanosecond that you've looked away? Then you're dreaming. Time tends to come away from its moorings in our dreams.

Materiality

When choosing a body part for a real test, choose an object or part of your body to use consistently as a reality test. That might be your mobile device, your car keys, or your hand or leg. You may even want to pinch yourself as you ask, "Am I dreaming?"

You can also try pushing the fingers of one hand into the palm of the other. Materiality – the solidity of objects – is a dead giveaway that you are, indeed, awake.

Choose your reality test and perform it several times per day, in concert with asking yourself if you're awake. Reality testing programs your mind to question the state of consciousness that presents itself. This will seep into your dream state when it becomes a habit.

Wake Back to Bed (WBTB)

The WBTB technique is exactly what it sounds like. You wake up and then, you go back to sleep.

There are many versions of WBTB but try this one first, as it's relatively uncomplicated:

- Set the alarm for five hours after you go to bed. This is the point in your sleep cycle at which you're more likely to be in REM or adjacent to it.
- When the alarm goes off, wake up and engage in an activity like reading or writing – something that requires full attention and alertness – for 20 - 30 minutes.
- After your wakeful time period has elapsed, go back to sleep.

Alertness is the defining trigger for lucid dreaming using this technique. Full alertness restores your conscious state, but being awakened before having your requisite night's sleep leaves you sleepy. The break in the sleep cycle starts the process. The alertness required to read or write sets the scene. Practicing WBTB renders you much more likely to experience a lucid dream.

Like reality testing, WBTB is a simple technique. It's also highly flexible, allowing you to tailor it to your individual needs. As with everything I'm sharing with you, I need to stress that you're unique and that what works perfectly for someone else may not have quite the same efficacy for you. You may need a longer wakeful period. You may need to set the alarm clock for a shorter or longer period. With WBTB, you have the flexibility to experiment and revise.

As you conclude your wakeful period, relax and go back to sleep but do so with the firm intention in your mind that you will be lucid dreaming. Suggestion is a powerful tool in this respect. Like affirmations, telling yourself that you are going to do something makes it far more likely that you will.

Its popularity among lucid dreamers means that you can find endless opportunities to discuss what your fellow lucid dreamers are doing in terms of WBTB online at the communities I've shared in the resources section at the end of the book. You'll find many lucid dreamers are only too happy to share their tips and tricks with you!

Best of all, WBTB is highly effective and involves very little effort.

Some lucid dreamers like to supplement WBTB with IMP (Impossible Movement Practice). Let's take a moment to see what this technique entails.

Impossible Movement Practice (IMP)

Daniel Love, the inventor of this induction technique, designed it to work with WBTB. IMP can be done just before you return to bed or at other times (before a nap or when awoken spontaneously when it's likely you'll return to REM sleep).

The idea is to visualize yourself performing an impossible physical movement. Hand movements are ideal for IMP. Before you begin, settle into the position you intend to fall asleep in, whether that's on your back or side. Now, visualize something like attempting to touch the back of your hand with the thumb on the same hand. It can't be done.

But by visualizing the impossible movement and focusing on it as you sleep, the imagery you have in your mind will endure as you fall asleep. Repeat the impossible movement constantly as you fall asleep.

As your consciousness transitions to sleep, you'll note a change in the quality of the movement. The imagined impossible movement takes on a tangible quality, producing the sensation that you're physically performing it.

The Counting Technique

It was Dr. Stephen LaBerge himself who invented this method of lucid dream induction. Counting is employed to initiate lucid dreaming. This is a simple but highly focused technique, so practitioners need to be laser-focused as they're transitioning to sleep. Concentration is the only skill required for this method, and if you're someone who struggles with imagery, the counting technique could be your ticket to lucid dreaming.

To use this technique, relax in a comfortable position and close your eyes. Count like this:

"1...I am dreaming, 2...I am dreaming, 3...I am dreaming." As you count, focus on the statement and the numbers you're counting. Continue until you've entered the dream space.

The counting induction technique has been highly successful when combined with **WBTB** and visualizing your habitual waking reality test. Its real power is in focus, which is important to employing this induction technique.

As your mind focuses, it's aware and conscious but at the same time relaxed due to the repetitive nature of the statement "I am dreaming" and the changing numbers. Some lucid dreamers like to count backward from 100. Choose what works best for you.

Mnemonic Induction Lucid Dreaming (MILD)

Again, Dr. Stephen LaBerge is the inventor of this technique. It was developed as part of his research toward a Ph.D. dissertation.

The word "mnemonic" means a pattern that helps us remember something. This might be a series of letters or associative cues which help us remember to do something important.

This is something we all do every day. We all have our own set of quirky, individual cues to remind us of tasks that need to be accomplished. Sometimes we give ourselves a "to do" list in the mirror as we brush our teeth or shave our faces. Some people just write the list down, as writing is a physical activity that helps to concretize a thought.

MILD's process is the same. You follow the steps (cues) that will remind you that you're dreaming. You'll also remind yourself to accomplish a goal in the dream state, whether that's behavioral, spiritual, or intellectual.

MILD is very successful when practiced during your regularly scheduled sleep time. For example, if you're awakening from a dream state, you take a moment to examine it and then, you apply what is known as the "three R's":

- Rescript
- Rehearse
- Remind

The three R's serve to remind you to be aware of the dream state when you go back to sleep. They set your intention for the lucid dreaming state of consciousness. Repeat them as many times as possible to instill confidence that you will enter lucid dreaming when you fall asleep.

Before we get into the details of our intention-supporting three R's, let's talk a little about "dream signs," as these figure in this technique as part of the rescripting portion.

A dream sign is simply an event, object, or place setting that is obviously beyond the material reality of waking life. For example, you may dream you're on the other side of the planet when you're in Newark, NJ, or Cranston, RI. You may dream that you're bald when you sport a full head of hair. Animals in your dreams may talk or have human faces, or their fur may be an odd color, like pink. These are all dream signs. We'll be talking more about items like objects and characters later on in the book, but dream signs are simply indications that the state of consciousness you're experiencing is a dream and not reality, and these are important, as they're signposts from your subconscious mind.

Details of the Three R's

Rescript: Waking up from the dream and remembering it, you need to think about how you'd like a dream to go in a lucid state of consciousness. Examine your dream for a dream sign. Then, choose the point of the dream at which one of these is present. Then say, "This is a dream."

After this point of the dream, re-organize the events you've identified to achieve a task that's meaningful to you.

Rehearse: Next, cast yourself back into the context of the dream you've awoken from. But this goes around; you'll be imagining the version that you've just rescripted from the point of the dream sign. As you do so, visualize lucidity and how the dream will unfold, rescripted by your waking mind. Repeat as necessary until you can see yourself clearly in the dream, as you remember that you are dreaming.

Reminder: Now that you've rescripted and rehearsed, it's time to remind yourself that when you fall asleep and enter the dream state that you will be aware that you're dreaming.

You can say something like, "This next dream I'll have will be lucid. I will recognize the dream signs as they come. They may be familiar or new, but I will know they are dream signs, and I will know that I'm dreaming when I see them."

Write this intention to suit yourself. Your intention may be much simpler. It might be more like, "My dream signs will remind me that I'm dreaming, and I will recognize them." Whatever you say, mean it. Have confidence that your intention is as real as the waking world. The more focused and confident you are, the more likely it is that MILD will work for you.

The wonderful thing about the MILD technique is that it can be applied to wakefulness. For example, remembering dreams you've had in the past can feed the technique, as these can also be rescripted and rehearsed to create a portal to lucid dreaming. You can also apply the technique to events.

For example, maybe you've had an altercation with someone recently that you believe might have been avoided had you approached the discussion differently. Rescript, rehearse, remind. Choose the inflection point (where things took a turn for the worst) as your dream sign and then change your behavior in the lucid dream. If you apply MILD to the event, you are enacting a useful, proactive aspect of lucid dreaming – that it can help us lead better, more productive, more peaceful lives. The applications are virtually endless!

Some Helpful MILD Tips

While this technique isn't complicated, it requires a lot of focus and intention. These tips will help you navigate that aspect of MILD.

Some practitioners find they fall asleep before completing the three R's. You know yourself, and you know how easily you can fall asleep. Propping yourself up in bed instead of lying down may work best, or even sitting on the edge of the bed as you rescript, rehearse and remind.

But what if you can't remember your dream? Simply choose another dream you can remember in detail and then practice using that dream. You can pretend the dream was lucid by applying the rescripting and rehearsing portions, applying them to the substitute dream.

The dream you wind up having doesn't strictly follow the trajectory you expect. That's okay. Dreams change, and setting them in stone isn't MILD's purpose. MILD deploys the imagery your mind has presented as an exercise to help you know that you're dreaming. This is the key – improving the likelihood that you'll be able to apply your intentions for lucid dreaming by recognizing the imagery.

When practicing the three R's, recall as much detail as possible, then repeat, repeat, repeat. Repetition and visualization and restoring the vividness of the dream in your mind should include the emotional landscape featured in the dream and your thoughts in that environment. This concretizes the action and allows you to grow your ability to revise your dreams and attain the lucidity you're seeking. Knowing that you're dreaming, being conscious of the fact you're conscious in the dream state, allows you to become proficient as a lucid dreamer.

Again, writing dreams down is highly effective due to the physical action of writing. Writing your rescripted version of dreams in your dream journal materializes them and provides a record of your progress, as well as allowing you to compare the original dream to the rescripted one.

The three R's are your partners in lucid dreaming. By learning to recognize dream signs, you're strengthening your mind and training it in a new world of awareness. In this awareness, you connect your conscious mind to the subconscious, enabling you to mine its riches.

And remember: The more you practice, the more able you'll be to enter the lucid dream state. Practice may not make perfect, but it most certainly does improve your ability to control your mind. No matter what else you believe you'll gain from lucid dreaming, controlling your own mind is a skill that reaps amazing rewards in the waking world. It's a life skill and one worth developing.

You need to practice MILD every night. You may prefer to take your time to build your confidence. But as you do, this framework for practicing MILD may be of use to you.

1. When the Lights Go Out

Go to bed with the intention of noticing wakefulness in the night. Remind yourself to recall the content of your dreams in detail when you wake up.

As you're falling asleep, apply the three R's to a dream you've had recently, recalling it as though it were lucid. Then tell yourself you'll be dreaming after you fall asleep. Let that statement of intention be the last thought you have to before falling asleep.

2. When You Wake Up at the Night

Be clear that you know you've woken up. Say it out loud. Then recall the dream and record it in your dream journal.

Again, use the three R's. Rescript and rehearse as though the dream were lucid. A recent dream can stand in if you haven't dreamed before awakening. Then, remind yourself – "I will remember that I'm dreaming."

3. When You Wake Up in the Morning

The first thing you do each morning should be to reach for that dream journal and write down every detail you can remember from your dream(s), including the emotional content and any thoughts you can remember.

Then, apply the three R's to the dream, rescripting and rehearsing it as though it were lucid. Finally, remind yourself that the next time you sleep, you will remember that you're dreaming.

In our next two chapters, we'll be talking about how to control your lucid dreams. In the first of these chapters, we'll discuss dream stabilization techniques. In the second, we'll talk about your dream body and how to get better acquainted with it.

Chapter Five: Dream Control I: Dream Stabilizing Techniques

One of the first things you need to understand about the art of lucid dreaming is that it's an art where mastery is attained through patience, practice, and an intense learning curve.

Part of that learning curve is coming to understand how lucid dreams may end sooner than we'd prefer. When lucid dreams "collapse," it can be frustrating and disappointing, so we will look at some reasons this happens and how we can apply techniques to stabilize lucid dreams.

One pitfall for beginning lucid dreamers is the thrill of the experience. Being lucid in the dreamscape can change physical conditions in your body, such as heart rate. When this happens, the lucid state of consciousness can rapidly become wakefulness and the dream – over before it can start! This is frustrating for lucid dreamers, especially those new to the practice. After putting a lot of time and energy into attaining the state of consciousness, it ends far too soon.

But some methods can assist you in staying in the lucid dream state, which we'll talk about here.

Let's review some excellent techniques for preventing the collapse of your lucid dreams, starting with some general advice about dream stabilization.

General Guidelines

Mindfulness (being aware of everything you're doing at the moment and of the people around you whose worlds your actions may affect) is one way to begin stabilizing your lucid dreams. Awareness itself is a hedge against your dream collapsing too quickly.

If your dream appears to be losing clarity (fading away), be aware of it. Signs of a loss of clarity are manifested in a loss of image quality or focus and color quality. Loss of detail is another sign. When you see these signs, your job is to integrate yourself into the dream fully. Touch what you see. Deliberately move your body through the dream. The more of your dream senses you engage with as the dream plays out, the more likely it is that clarity will be restored and the dream won't collapse. You can also verbally demand that clarity be restored by saying something like, "I need clarity!" or "High def. Now!" And mean it! The intention is everything with the statements you make to induce lucid dreaming or stabilize a lucid dream. Demand clarity firmly and assertively to prevent the collapse of your lucid dream.

And, if you feel as though you've awakened in the dream, perform the real test that works best for you to ensure it's not a false awakening. It's often the case that you're dreaming that you've woken up, so test the sensation against reality.

Your imagination is a huge part of successful lucid dreaming. And engaging with the dream is a function that requires all the images you have. Your senses are powerful, even in the dreamscape, so go beyond seeing. Engage your other senses, actively seeking to "sense" other features of the dream.

Also be as active as possible in the dream. Dance, walk, climb a nearby tree, do some sit-ups. Physical action in the dreamscape instigated by the dreamer is one of the best ways to keep your dream from collapsing (see spinning and a physical touch below).

Why Do Lucid Dreams Collapse?

I began lucid dreaming when I was quite young. These experiences continued into adulthood until I finally decided it was time to investigate the phenomenon and see if it could induce this state of consciousness.

The problem with my spontaneous lucid dreams is the one we're discussing in this chapter – collapse. The more I thought about the fact that I was having an unusual type of dream, the shorter the dream would be. Once, I recall waking up from a nap. I was lying in bed. I could see the food on my bed and the other side of my room. It was daylight, so I felt I was awake. But then I realized that other details of what I was experiencing weren't possible in waking consciousness, like the multi-colored, translucent orbs floating around the room.

Dead Giveaway!

When I realized I was dreaming, I could remain in the dream, and to this day, I remember it vividly. This was the dream that got my fascination with lucid dreaming started. If you're reading this book, you've probably had a similar experience.

Lucid dreaming is a thrilling experience, and sometimes, we get so thrilled, we crash our dream. That's completely understandable, as experiencing the phenomenon is genuinely exciting. But the point here is to extend the lucid dream, and getting overheated about the experience is one surefire way to shut it down.

So, a foundational skill is to remember to stay calm. As Larry David would sagely counsel, "Curb Your Enthusiasm!" Remind yourself that you need to be as calm as possible not to disrupt lucidity when you dream.

Next, let's look at some popular lucid dream stabilization techniques.

Spinning

Stephen LaBerge also invented the "spinning" technique for preventing lucid dream collapse. Spinning is a form of visualization specifically tailored to lucid dreamers.

Visualize yourself spinning around and around, like a Sufi mystic or a ballerina doing a pirouette. Spin fast or slow – it doesn't matter. Your speed is the one you find most useful for stabilizing your dream.

The focus of visualizing yourself spinning has the effect of centering you in the physical act, which sharpens your perception. You may also find that details of the dream change post-spin. For example, if you were outside, pre-spin, you may find yourself inside, post-spin. You may even want to visualize a change of venue intending to switch your setting deliberately.

While spinning (or performing any of the other stabilization techniques described here), saying the words "Lucidity now!" serve your intention in the stabilization. As you are learning throughout this book, statements like this layer a physical action (speaking) with an intellectual action, creating a more robust framework for it. It's a bit like writing things down or saying things aloud adds a dimension of the "real" in the physicality of the act.

Physical Touch

The physical, once again, is a powerful means of correcting lucid dream collapse. One popular technique for achieving this is to simply rub your hands together.

Rubbing your hands together as part of your preparation for lucid dreaming at the induction stage and then, throughout the lucid dream, creates a touchstone in the physical that sharpens perception in the dream space, heightening awareness of details you might otherwise miss. By having a stabilizing action-ready involving physical top – even pinching yourself – your lucid dream is much less likely to collapse.

Focusing on a Physical Detail

Because of the nature of dreams, one of the most reliable ways to stabilize a dreamscape is to focus on something that will not change. Your hands, for example. Intentionally looking at your hands and realizing that they are yours and unchanged in the dreamscape creates a point of stability. Carlos Castaneda, famous for his books about the mythical figure, Don Juan, and this figure's teachings, used this technique in his lucid dreaming adventures.

But physical details can be anything from the ground you're standing on to the bed you're lying in: the concrete and the real anchor you, not only in your consciousness but in the dreamscape.

Math

You need not be a mathlete to perform simple mathematical equations like 2 plus 2 equals 4—the very act of forcing your mind to perform mathematical sum centers you in the dreamscape.

Even a simple sum engages your brain to perform one of its higher functions, thus building consciousness.

Staring at the Ground

Your body isn't the only stable feature of your dream. Another is the surface you're standing on. Unless your lucid dream features some type of earth-shattering catastrophe, looking down at the floor or the ground you're standing on is a way to stop your dream from collapsing.

Sensing an imminent collapse, simply stare down and focus on the reality and stability of your feet on the ground or floor. If the floor collapses or the earth opens beneath you, switch your focus to the sky or ceiling! Whatever is a stable feature in your dream is something you can stare at intently to re-establish a clear and compelling dreamscape.

Shake Your Head

Physical actions taken in a lucid state of consciousness have the power to prolong your dreams. The very physicality of actions like spinning, rubbing your hands, and shaking your head has the potential to ground you in the dreamscape.

Start slowly, intentionally, and shaking your head from side to side. As you do so, you may find it helpful to combine this action with a statement about clarity, like "high def., now" or "I demand clarity." The intention is self-talk, which communicates a clear message to your subconscious.

Focus on Your Breathing

We've already talked about staying calm in a lucid state, and breathing is a good way to achieve that. Those of you following my preparation advice will already have familiarized yourself with breathing as a means of centering yourself in meditation. Breathing works the same way in lucid dreaming.

Focus on the act of inhaling and exhaling, slowing your breathing until you feel the dream has stabilized. Again, breathing is a physical action. Usually unconscious, when you focus on it, breathing becomes something you control. As you control your breathing, you control your dreamscape.

An Experiment

In 1995, Stephen LaBerge wrote of an experiment conducted by members of the Lucidity Institute (founded by Dr. LaBerge) at Sanford University.

The experiment examined the effectiveness of the spinning, physical actions, and another technique, termed simply "going with the flow" (which describes continuing with the action in the dream as it threatened to collapse, as though everything was in order). Following is what they discovered the efficacy of these methods.

The subjects in the experiment were instructed to repeat the words "the next scene will be a dream" as they were performing the technique being tested. The experiment implicated 34 test subjects. Of these, 53% tested all three techniques listed.

The results are certainly of interest in our discussion of dream stabilization. Spinning increased the odds of the lucid dream continuing by just over 4%. Rubbing the hands together increased the odds by 7% and going with the flow by a negligible percentage.

These results, informally achieved in a very small sample, are not representative, but they indicate that the physical component involved in rubbing the hands together had a much stronger effect than visualizing a physical action (spinning). It was also concluded that the visualization of spinning disrupted the visual aspects of the dream. This may have contributed to destabilization sometimes, rather than reducing the probability of the dream collapsing.

I look forward to furthering research from this source on these induction techniques.

Time Loses Its Meaning in Dreams

Whether it's lucid dreaming or the kind of dreams we're all accustomed to having, time loses its meaning as we dream.

It's difficult to say how long dreams last in real-time. Sometimes, they seem to go on for hours when we've only been dreaming for a few minutes. Nighttime dreams are usually brief, lasting for several minutes. But dreams in the morning, just before we wake up, can last up to 30 minutes. As your sleep cycles come to an end, REM sleep becomes more profound, allowing extended lucid dreaming in the final REM period of the cycle with the possibility of lucid dreams occurring in periods before and after the REM section. In the lucid dream space, when you understand how to control the dreams you'll be having, they can last much longer.

As you've observed, we're following a logical progression toward establishing your ability to dream lucidly. Something you need to remember is this process may not be rushed. Your mind must be prepared for lucidity to be achieved. While it's tempting to jump ahead, skip steps, and cut corners, those practices won't get you where you want to be.

Approach lucid dreaming as a discipline you're learning. Like any other discipline, practice is key. Talent will only get you so far. If you're not willing to do the work, your talent will never be realized, as it will remain undeveloped. Many of you reading will feel an affinity for lucid dreaming, and that's great. Some of you will have experienced lucidity spontaneously. That doesn't mean that you'll automatically be able to dream lucidly just because you want to.

A previous experience of lucid dreaming also doesn't mean that you'll be any more successful than any other novice lucid dreamer. You need to learn all the preparation steps and components of the lucid dreaming experience before you can derive from the experience everything it has to give you. And part of that is understanding why your dreams collapse and how to stop them from doing so.

Maybe you're content with something close to what's possible. But if you think about it, that's just second-best. To get to where you command the lucid dream experience, you need to be meticulous in your approach by following the advice in this book and elsewhere in your studies.

Before moving on to our next chapter, let's review some of the key techniques outlined in this chapter.

Spinning: With spinning, your mind projects motion into the dream to stop it from collapsing. Sometimes, invoking spinning may stop the dream you're in (which is collapsing anyway) and propel you into a new dream.

Physical Touch: Touching your body or objects in the dream tethers you to the dream space, having the potential to slow or halt the collapse. It's the action that counts here.

Focusing on Details: The act of focusing on specific details of your dream connects the dreamer to the substance of the dream.

Math: Performing a simple mathematics sum activates brain function and consciousness, putting you back in charge of the dream.

Staring at the ground: Save instances of the ground swallowing you or the floor you're standing on collapsing; staring at the ground connects you to a physical component of the dream that's stable, just as your body is. That stability influences the dream's overall stability, influenced by your focus on it.

Focus Your Breathing: The deliberate inhalations and exhalations practiced in meditation constitute a physical act brought forward into the conscious mind by intention. When we expressly think about an unconscious bodily function, we control it. By controlling it, we control the dreamscape via conscious intention, just as we're mining our subconscious in the act of lucidity.

Before we move on, I cannot stress enough the value of moving into your lucid dreaming experiences with a calm mental landscape. Being overexcited is natural, but if you enter lucidity in that mental state, your chances of success are limited. Much of the art of lucid dreaming is concerned with the dreamer's ability to control themselves – their reactions, mindset, and physical responses. There is a "Zen" to lucid dreaming that applies to virtually every area of your life.

You could say that lucid dreaming is really about equanimity. Equanimity is the ability to see everything that happens in life as having equal value. Failures, for example, are no less valuable than victories. This is as true in life as it is in lucid dreaming, as I'm sure most readers will agree.

When we fail, we not only try again, we learn. And in that learning are the seeds of success. Don't be discouraged by your lucid dreams collapsing or not achieving lucidity on the first try or even the first several tries. As you move along the path to lucidity, you'll understand what it asks of you. Often, what's asked is needed change to a facet of our personality that's somehow impeding our progress in other areas.

You are learning. Give yourself the grace and time to approach lucid dreaming respectfully. You are a supplicant at the feet of the cosmos, petitioning for entry to a world of wonder. Worlds like that don't open their doors readily. But those who knock with intention and humility will enter.

In our next chapter, we'll be talking about your dream body, what it is and how you will become better acquainted with it. So, let's move on to the next step in our journey toward lucidity.

Chapter Six: Dream Control II: Getting Accustomed to Your Dream Body

"If you must sleep through a third of your life, must you sleep through your dreams, too?"

Stephen LaBerge

As you may have guessed, the body you experience in your dreams is rather different from your waking body. It's still you. It's just you with abilities you don't have in the waking world.

Many of us have flown in our dreams or have run like the wind. We've jumped incredible distances and scaled the otherwise unscalable walls of skyscrapers. Just as time has no meaning in our dreams, neither do the waking limitations of our bodies.

But the experience of the human body in a lucid dream is very different. With this state of consciousness, the body takes on these fantastical qualities but in a very different way. So, what we'll talk about in this chapter is how to feel comfortable in your body and how to get used to the marvelous things it can do, as well as the sensations you'll experience as you dream.

The Lessons of the Body in Lucid Dreams

In many real ways, modernity has robbed humans of their own bodies. Does that sound crazy? Well, let's talk about it for a moment.

Many of us spend a lot of time in vehicles, whether private or public (taxis, transit). We tend to avoid walking at all costs. We live in homes replete with appliances to make our lives easier, from toasters to washing machines. We don't even need to wash the dishes ourselves anymore.

And then, there are the screens. Interactive screens that connect us to other people via telecommunications, which entertain and inform us, are ubiquitous in modern life, so we spend a lot of time sitting and scrolling or talking or working.

All these things and many others have imparted a kind of false redundancy to our bodies. We think of them as vehicles for our inner persons. But without the body, how are we recognizable? How do we move from place to place? How do you embrace those we love or even lock the front door when we leave our homes?

Modernity has put the human body in a kind of suspension. Many of us spend little time thinking about our bodies, what they need, or that they're time-limited resources that will decline to the point of death one day.

But the body is more than a vessel. Maurice Merleau-Ponty once wrote of the human body as a "borderland" that provided us with the means to "have a world." More than a mere interface, the human body is a complex sum of our personhood, providing those we encounter with numerous clues about who we are, from the expressions on our faces to our state of physical health. And yet, because of the convenient world we live in, we neglect our physical beings, as crucial as they are to our continuing existence.

Lucid dreaming is a portal to a new way of thinking about our bodies and what they mean to us, existentially. The lessons of our body in lucid dreaming encompass reflecting on the energetic superhighways that form it and how energy moves through them. But we can also learn about where our bodies need to be healed.

Learning about how our bodies work in the lucid dream space, where they're light, capable, and endlessly flexible, can have the effect of reconnecting us to these amazing earthly expressions of our humanity. And in that enfleshment, we can approach the sacred nature of what living as an incarnated being means, perhaps teaching us new, profound truths we might otherwise never be privy to.

In those dreams in which our bodies aren't featured, we can learn about existence beyond this life and what that could mean when our physical existence ends.

Preparing Your Body for Lucid Dreaming

Has modernity robbed you of the intimate relationship with your body that should, by nature, be present? Do you feel weirdly dissociated? Do you think of your body as a bit of a pain in the rear end?

Then you're one of many. The nature of modernity has made the human body almost a shameful thing to have. We're annoyed by its constant needs and demands. We fear the diseases that can compromise it, getting hurt or permanently disabled. Modern philosophy has even posited a future in which humans may become disembodied as an evolutionary necessity (Ray Kurzweil).

We've talked about preparing your mind for lucid dreaming, but as we're now talking about the dream body and its manifestation in lucid dreaming, we should also briefly discuss preparing your body.

You're going to be learning about a version of your body that exists in the lucid dreaming state of consciousness, so reacquainting yourself with the body you're accustomed to is not only a good idea; it's the basis for the learning curve you're about to scale. Knowing your dream body and becoming accustomed to it starts with re-establishing an intentional connection to your own body, its quirks, and capabilities.

Choose a Form of Movement

I'm deliberately avoiding the "e" word here. I know that many tremble when this word is mentioned, so we'll use the word "movement" for the purposes of this book. We're not talking about whipping you into shape. We're talking about getting to know your waking body to prepare yourself for lucid dreaming.

What I suggest to readers unaccustomed to thinking about your physical beings is that you choose a form of movement you feel not only comfortable with but enjoy doing. Dance might be the right fit for you. But you might also feel attracted to Tai Chi (the gentle repetition of movements designed to condition and stretch muscles) or Yoga. Maybe you like riding a bicycle.

Whichever form of movement you choose to pursue, the point is living in the movement as you perform it. Here are some questions to ask yourself as you're practicing the form of movement you choose to prepare yourself for lucid dreaming:

- Which muscles are most prominent as I move?
- Is my body properly aligned?
- Does something hurt?
- Is my heart pumping more quickly?
- Am I thirsty?

Ask yourself questions in direct relation to the movement and how it makes your body feel and perform. This is not "exercise." This is a movement to center you in the reality of your body, in its waking incarnation. By reconnecting with how your physical being responds to movement, you'll come to remember things about your body you may have forgotten, like how good it feels to move intentionally, for example, if that's not usually part of your life.

I will not tell you to make movement a regular part of your life. I don't have to. You'll figure that out for yourself! And as you do, you'll be connecting your body with the brain that runs the whole show. That connection is always present, subconsciously. But intentionally provoking yourself to recognize your body as you and not some needy, annoying crackerjack box will prepare you for the miracle of lucid dreaming. Your waking body and your dream body are both you. But your dream body, informed by your acceptance of and recognition of your waking body, will be so much more appreciated when you've prepared for the experience by re-establishing your intellectual connection to it.

People with physical disabilities most certainly enjoy a dream body unbound by the physical limitations of their waking body, just as we all do. But the effect is much more dramatic, as the dream body performs activities that their waking bodies don't. Again, that's true of all of us to an extent. Knowing your body and feeling connected to it is one of the most effective ways to ensure we remain tethered to reality and its concrete nature as we're journeying in this state of consciousness. Being aware of your body will also project your conscious relationship with it into the dreamscape, tipping you off to the fact that you are dreaming.

The Mini-Me Proposal

Doctor of Psychology, Judith Koppehele-Gossel, of Bonn University in Germany, published the study's findings, A template model of embodiment while dreaming: Proposal of a mini-me, in September 2016. These results appeared in the journal, Consciousness and Cognition.

The study results indicate that our subconscious's dream body bears little in common with our waking body. This finding was underlined because disabled study participants rendered similar results to those with no such physical disabilities. The dream bodies of the differently able present as normative, unimpeded. This led implicated researchers to propose that what the dream body truly is, is a type of mini-me (as seen in the Austin Powers films, in which the character, Dr. Evil, is accompanied by a tiny person who is his "mini-me").

The dream body, the study concludes, capable of feats like flying and walking through walls, is disembodied in our waking realities. Its reality in dreams is disconnected from the physical self, existing as a template of our enfleshed selves.

This conclusion was reached using physical control, namely

placing a red dot on the participants' right arm. Researchers instructed participants to be aware of the mark on their arms before entering the dreamscape. But it was found when participants reported back on their dreams that this physical control didn't appear in reports. Even when the control mechanism was adjusted by asking participants to focus intently on the arm, the red dot was focused on for 2 minutes before going to sleep, and the results were the same. This indicates that the dream body is a mini-me generated by the subconscious, taking on the generally accepted form of the able human body. Differently able participants were normatively able in their dreams.

Stripped down to its physical function, the dream body is a mini-me, in that it is not the fullness of who you are. Or perhaps it's more apt to say that the dream body is the fullness of the subconscious expectations of our bodies or desires for them. Unaffected by the physical reality of your waking body, the dream body operates in the dream state as a representation or prototype.

The "mini-me" proposal goes a long way toward understanding why we can perform such amazing physical feats in the dreamscape. It is not our body. It is the body of our dreams and in our dreams, existing nowhere else outside that context.

The red dot placed on participants' arms proves that the dream body is differentiated from the waking body. Were that not the case, the red dot would have shown up in participant dreams in one way or another, but there was no indication of any kind that it did.

The study's key finding was that the dream is not influenced by methodologies of focused attention or the power of suggestion (like, for example, repeating to yourself that you want to dream about your arm and the red dot on it).

Dr. Koppehele-Gossel noted that the study indicated that the dream body is not analogous to the waking body but is rather a minimalist representation, which led researchers to apply the term "mini-me." The dream body, then, is a separate reality generated by the subconscious.

Most dreamers see little of their bodies in their dreams. But this book is about lucid dreaming, so let's move into examining the dream body in that context. Koppehele-Gossel hopes to explore the further embodiment of dreaming and how it relates to various states of consciousness. Again, I'm looking forward to reading more about this fascinating sub-area of study.

The Lucid Dream Body

The dream body of conventional dreams is of interest to us as we discuss the art of lucidity. While most dreamers don't "see" their dream bodies, they're aware of their performing physical feats, so action drives the reference rather than observation.

In lucid dreaming, observation accompanied by lucid consciousness drives the action. At least that's what we hope will happen when we enter the lucid dream space.

But to "see" the dream body, we must employ all the weapons in our lucid dreaming arsenal. Part of that is connecting to our physical selves in wakefulness, knowing how our bodies feel, what they look like, and what they're capable of. That connection is important because it informs the lucid dream itself. Reality and the dreamscape work in a creative synergy, which we are talking about in terms of how our bodies look and behave in lucidity.

While offering a fascinating new way for researchers to study consciousness, the mini-me proposal doesn't impact the divergent experience of lucid dreaming. Because we're talking about a different form of consciousness, the body we use in lucid dreaming is as vulnerable to suggestion as anything else we encounter in our dreams once we've become proficient.

Reality Checking and the Dream Body

I've emphasized the importance of adding physical awareness to intellectual awareness in this chapter, as it's just another avenue for testing the reality you're in. You may add to your repertoire of reality checks, "Is this my body?" You can ask the question of any part of your body or apply it to the whole organism. You can then say, "I will fly now," "I will climb this sheer wall," and other affirming statements about your physical capacity in the lucid dreamscape.

Because in a lucid dream, your dream body can do whatever you want it to, depending on how you direct and orchestrate your activity in the dream space. And we already know that reality checks with a physical basis are some of the most effective (pressing the palm of one hand with the fingers of the opposite hand and other physical checks).

A recurring dream I've experienced since my teens see me running from an unseen threat. When I'd reached the part of the dream in which I'm running from this threat, the dream usually ended with me trying to outrun whatever it was and waking myself up. But as time went by, I recognized the dream and realized I could change the outcome. As I ran into the dreamscape, I realized that I could *will myself* to fly, and suddenly, I was flying. The question was answered before it was asked, as I instinctively knew that I could fly if I so willed it.

That is how lucid consciousness works with the dream body in the dreamscape. You drive the action to achieve the effect you desire. In my example, the desire was to outrun an unidentified threat by taking to the air. It doesn't matter what your waking body can or can't do in its context of consciousness. Your dream body is yours to control, to enjoy, and to send on adventures you've never imagined – even if that adventure is taking a flight to avoid a threat! Whatever your desire, you can achieve it with your awareness.

By developing a more conscious, intentional relationship with your physical person, you'll gain greater confidence in directing the action of your dream body and understanding the material capabilities of your waking body grounds and centers you in it. This tethers you to the real while opening the door to union with your mysterious and endlessly able dream body. Whether it's flying, walking through walls, or being invisible, your mind is the birthplace of your dream body. But its relationship to your material body provides the concrete ground of your insight into how you can use it in the dreamscape.

Remember that the body is a holistic reality. What we project into the dreamscape about our material body is a function of the mind that directs all body functions, both conscious and unconscious. Living in the integrated wonder of the body elevates your self-knowledge and apprehension of what it means to be human.

In short, the dream body is your psychological projection of the real thing. It's not so much a "mini-me" as a hologram directed by your will and imagination. Like your waking body, the dream body dances to your tune. Even the normally unconscious action of breathing can be manipulated to serve you better.

You and only you are the dream body's progenitor. You choose the song on the jukebox, the dance partner, and the dance hall. When you understand yourself as an integrated being or a unitive reality, you will find a friend, a facilitator, and a projection of some of your most cherished hopes in the dream body.

In our next chapter, we'll discover symbols and objects that appear in our lucid dreams, what they mean, why they appear, and how to create symbols and objects in the dream space. We'll also look at some examples of how these items operate in the dreamscape.

Chapter Seven: Dream Objects and Symbols

This chapter is one of the most psychologically interesting in the book, dealing with the objects and symbols we encounter in the lucid dream space.

But we don't only see them in this state of consciousness, of course. They're all around us. The study of semiotics instructs as to the meaning behind them in the contexts of both lucid and conventional dreaming.

A sign holds within it the global meaning of symbols and how they operate. For example, the "don't walk" sign is interpreted globally as meaning "stay on the curb, or you'll walk into oncoming traffic," which is the symbolic meaning of the sign beyond the directive "don't walk." The symbol is part of the sign, indicating the fullness of the meaning on a more in-depth level.

Carl Jung, the great psychiatrist, and psychotherapist founded the discipline of analytical psychology, positing a system of archetypes (similar to the "forms" of Greek philosophy) which drive, inform and underlie human behavior. Jung thought of symbols as holistic, "living bodies," following the Aristotelian theory of forms, which states that the symbol doesn't exist independently but by virtue of the object it represents. Plato believed the opposite, that forms were a universal abstraction existing outside the bounds of objects.

Jung's archetypes exist as common themes in human life and the imagery associated with them. He believed that archetypes arose from the collective unconscious, producing commonly shared meanings across numerous cultures. Often seen in art and religious expression, archetypes also appear in our dreams, and lucid dreaming is not excluded. As a psychiatrist, Jung labeled these the Self, the Persona, the Shadow, and the Anima/Animus, as the theory of forms he developed addressed the human psyche. These four archetypes form an umbrella over the 12 Jungian archetypes, which are a subject for another book, but I hope you'll be encouraged to meet them and come to understand them as part of your lucid dreaming journey. They can be very useful for those of us plumbing our unconscious minds.

Jungian Archetypes

Jung's hypothesis states that the primitive, pre-history shared by all humans is the source of the archetypes we globally share. Despite cultural differences, imperatives, and barriers, these archetypes are part of us, lurking in the collective unconscious as a common human legacy.

Let's review the four archetypes mentioned in the last section.

The Self

The self is the unifying principle of human experience. This is the ground of our consciousness and the defining locus of discovering who we are and then *being that person.*

The Persona

The Persona is our public presentation to others, essentially a "mask" we wear. This mask represents conformity and our universal desire to be liked and accepted. The true self is mediated by its presentation, in which it's veiled.

The Anima/Animus

This archetype represents dimorphic, biological sex but as a mirror image of the sex opposite our own. All women and all men have traits deemed either "feminine" or "masculine" in the social construct of gender.

Because men and women have lived with one another for all of history, the lines of socially prescribed gender are, in Jung's model, blurred by familiarity. The Animus (masculine) subconsciously shares the Anima's (feminine) traits, while the Anima reciprocates, sharing masculine traits.

The Shadow

Analogous to Freud's id, the Shadow is our animal nature. The archetype symbolizes the freedom of "wildness," unimpeded by conformity. But it also represents the human potential (even propensity) for destruction. This is the side of us that teeters on the brink of savagery.

As you can see, just from these simple explanations of the archetypes shared by all humans, there is much to unpack here, especially in light of lucid dreaming. A question about the true nature of the self and its expression in the world is immediately raised. What mask do we wear in our daily lives to conform to what's widely considered socially "acceptable." How do we stunt our potential as men and women due to prohibitions about "acceptable" behavior of the two sexes attached to gender constructs? How does our Shadow archetype manifest in our lives? Are we in control of it?

And finally, Jungian archetypes ask us to look at the Self to determine if we live our lives to their fullest potential. This is a key function of lucid dreaming – in the dream space, we can ask ourselves the questions that remove blockages and old ideas about the significance of our persons and the lives we live. Stereotypes and prescribed behaviors are often behind the reason some people feel stuck in their lives.

Jung's archetypes speak to us from the beginning of the 20th Century. While never as widely disseminated as Freud's ideas, Jung's ideas continue to influence psychology, culture, the arts, film, music, and numerous other sectors. Unfortunately, the absence of a biological basis for Jungian archetypes has marginalized the framework to a degree. Jung's archetypes continue to stand as a portal to self-reflection and improvement, and that's why we're here.

Now that we know a little about how Jung viewed the human mind as part of a global collective unconscious, let's talk about objects and symbols. Specifically why they appear in lucid dreams and how science perceives these manifestations.

The Object in the Dreamscape

Objects appearing in lucid dreams might have special significance to the dreamer. They're different for everyone, and when they mean something to you, you'll know.

A teddy bear from your childhood may suddenly be present. That teddy bear may be a symbol of comfort to you. To someone else, it may be an object which symbolizes a traumatic event.

And that's the thing about objects in dreamscapes – they're not always there as "themselves." They're often a sign, indicating a deeper symbolic meaning to the dreamer. What's comforting for one dreamer might be an unpleasant reminder of trauma to another.

The object represents a period of your life or an incident, but it's important to remember that objects in lucid dreams aren't the actual object, so if you believe you've gotten your childhood teddy bear back because you've seen it in the dream space - no. This immaterial sign symbolizes a reality in your life that is perhaps unaddressed, poorly remembered, or a reminder of something (whether pleasant or unpleasant). More than anything, objects in all dreams - not only lucid - represent their counterparts in the material world and significant events in which they've been featured.

Some objects in the dreamscape have more than one meaning - one that's personal to the dreamer and another that's a global, semiotic translation of the object's meaning.

For example, you dream of a cushion embroidered with a comforting slogan - "There's no place like home." You may remember the cushion from your own life, and upon awakening, you remember it was a cushion in the front room of the home you shared with a former spouse. You don't associate the object with the slogan or general interpretation of a cushion in a dream. The general interpretation of a cushion or pillow in a dream is that of comfort and safety from harm.

But in your dream, that interpretation changes dramatically. Your experience of the cushion, even with the comforting slogan, is not associated with comfort or safety. You remember the cushion as a symbol of the truth of your now-defunct marriage - that home was not a comfortable or safe place to be because of what went on between you and your former spouse.

The lucid dream provides an opportunity regarding objects which appear as reminders of negative instances in the past or in your former life. They're presenting themselves in the dreamscape as opportunities. Again, those opportunities rely on the object's significance to you. A negative association with the dreamed object is usually a matter crying out for resolution. With the personal association of the cushion outlined, the matter would most superficially be a failure to find closure with a psychologically damaging past. Dreaming of such a sinister cushion, with its generally innocuous embroidered slogan, would indicate that you have some work to do to free yourself of a past that's continuing to damage you. You may even have Post-Traumatic Stress Disorder, needing treatment.

Like the teddy bear, universal meanings applied to objects in dreams are helpful in many instances. In others, they can prove frustrating when you're seeking to accurately interpret the message of a dream.

What Science Says About Visual Imagery (Including Objects)

In May 2013, a group of researchers in Kyoto, Japan, published their study on dreaming in the Journal of Science. Entitled "Neural Decoding Of Visual Imagery During Sleep," researchers sought to produce a model for predicting what people saw in their dreams, using "...an MRI, a computer model and thousands of images from the internet", according to an account in Smithsonian Magazine, dated April 4, 2014. Ultimately, researchers predicted the contents of three subjects' dreams with 60% accuracy.

How researchers achieved this is the real story. Even though the study addressed conventional and not lucid dreams, the processes involved in the production of dreams in the human brain are of greatest interest to us.

The study stemmed from the idea that our brains follow a certain pattern in their responses to visual imagery. With time, that hypothesis can produce an algorithm capable of matching the patterns of the brain's responses to various categories of visuals. While the study of this hypothesis about imagery and the brain has been approached before, it's only been conducted on subjects who were awake. The Kyoto study looks at the sleeping brain.

The study focused on 3 participants. Each spelled off 3-hour sleeping "shifts" in an MRI. Conducted over ten days, the study wired the three subjects with EEG (electroencephalography) to track the brain's electrical activity. This was used to show the stage in the sleep cycle participants were in. Interestingly, researchers were most interested in non-REM sleep (which occurs shortly after you fall asleep), using this cycle as the focus of their study.

Subjects were monitored until they'd entered stage 1 of the sleep cycle (as described) above, then awakened to describe their dreams to researchers, who performed this protocol 200 times over the 10-day course of the study.

Ingeniously, researchers made a note of the 20 most common types of imagery seen among the subjects (i.e., person, building, vase), then conducted searches for images on the internet that corresponded to these 20 categories.

The images were shown to study participants while awake and on the MRI scanner. The readings for the resulting readouts were then compared to readings from the subjects as they dreamed of the corresponding items. By doing so, researchers could pinpoint patterns of activity in the brain connected to a specific visual, rather than patterns that have nothing at all to do with the visuals – which are simply about the state of consciousness in sleep.

The data collected from participants about the types of objects seen in their dreams and the MRI readout showing their brains' responses were fed to a learning algorithm (Machine Learning). The algorithm was able to refine and improve its model for predicting the imagery seen by participants in their dreams based on the data.

The study participants returned to the MRI to apply the new algorithm, testing its accuracy. Videos were generated that produced image sets (as sourced on the Internet) and by choosing the most likely object from the list of 20 most common objects seen by participants in their dreams.

While exceeding "chance," the new prediction model wasn't perfect, but neither is 60% accuracy too shabby for a predictive model being tested on sleeping subjects!

The algorithm proved to be more accurate when identifying visuals from different categories of images. Within the category, results were much less reliable.

I think it's important to stress this study provides concrete evidence that our dreams point to the truth of what Carl Jung was talking about in his explorations of the human mind. There are archetypal objects and symbols we all know – without knowing how or why. These represent a shared psychological, emotional, and spiritual bond between all those who dream. Our dreams, featuring these archetypes, point to the existence of the collective unconscious rather pointedly.

The Kyoto study's researchers hold this study up as a possible first mover into the science of dream analysis, which is exciting news for all dreamers, lucid or otherwise.

I hope readers can see the potential with respect to lucid dreaming, which runs both ways. While it can serve to describe the brain activity involved in lucid dreaming, it also has the potential to serve science with a more specific understanding of what happens in the brain during sleep.

In other words, while what we've said above about personalization and global meaning stands on its own, the symbolic nature of objects and the semiotic arising from them is a universal reality, transcending cultures as prototypes of our collective, human experience.

That is how deeply important our dreams are. The dream state is a rarefied psychological ambiance in the brain that's inadequately studied by the scientific community. As the study discussed above attests, science is beginning to see the value of more actively pursuing the vast storehouse of information available to us in sleep research.

Sleep is the subconscious playground of the human mind, working out our daily challenges, taunting us for our failures, and urging us toward our victories. But in the lucid state, dreams have the potential to do so much more.

To conclude this chapter, we'll talk about an esoteric element of lucid dreaming – spawning objects, how it works, and what the practice can do. I've hinted at it earlier in this chapter in the teddy bear/cushion discussion about personalization.

Spawning Objects (Creating/Manifesting)

As a kid, I had a recurring dream that a little man in a cape was chasing me down the scarlet-carpeted corridors of an old hotel. I remember the paneled walls, the light sconces, and the open window at the end of the hall in the dream.

I also remember being aware that I was dreaming as I got older, but the dream occurred for many years without that knowledge. I believe it stems from an incident in childhood, during which I have chased off someone's lawn (as most children have been at one time or another). This neighbor was a small, older man with a ferocious dislike of children. He didn't wear a cape, but in my dream, I reinvented him. I believed him to be a villain – a sawed-off, unreasonably offended vampire. The lining of the cape was red.

I created the hotel as a way to make the angry little man chase me eternally. Yes, as a child, I enjoyed misadventure in the name of justice, only in the theater of my dreams. The dream, though, would always end before I reached the end of the hall and went through the open window.

I can't remember the year or how old I was, but one night, I was able to reach the end of the hall and throw myself out the window, instinctively knowing that I would then fly away from the runty Dracula wannabe. Without even understanding how I'd done it, I resolved the childhood memory of fear, rejection for unknown reasons, and the sense that violence was imminent. And how did that happen? I was just a kid.

There is no mind on earth more prone to fantasy than the mind of a child. Children also know that belief is at the heart of all success. They dream, create, and manifest without the inhibitions of adulthood to get in their way.

And if you're ready to create/manifest/spawn objects in your dream, the most important skill you can learn is that of believing you can do it. The truth is that you are already know-how. I knew how as a kid. I just didn't know what to call it or that it wasn't something everyone else was doing. I just did it.

But you're new to the art of lucid dreaming, so here's a technique you can learn to help establish the belief in your mind that spawning objects – even people (although they're more difficult) – is within your ability.

It is. You've just forgotten that it is because you live in the "rational" world of adulthood, in which dreaming, fantasizing, and creating are too often viewed with disapproval, if not open hostility.

Three-Step Method

Done while you're awake, the three-step method allows you to plan your manifestations.

The first step is to focus deeply on the object you're trying to spawn/create/manifest in your dream. Choose something significant to you – a favorite coffee mug, for example. For step 2, think about how the object makes you feel. Are you happy when you take it off the shelf and walk to the coffeemaker with it? Or are you throwing that coffee mug at someone or something in a frustrated rage?

Step 3 is to choose an environment in which to encounter the coffee mug in your dream, visualizing what you're doing. Follow this process several times on the day you're planning a lucid dream session. Remember to "believe" that your object will manifest, with belief in the power of your mind and its aptitudes.

As you're dream planning, don't forget to manifest first one object, then many more, that the object you choose for your first spawn should have a very individual resonance for you. Choosing a universal symbol is fine. That can work. But personally connecting to a specific item is a much more effective methodology, especially if you keep believing in your success front of mind.

In our next chapter, we'll talk about characters and the encounters you'll have with them in the lucid dream space.

Lucid Dreaming Activities

Chapter Eight: Dream Characters and Encounters

The characters we meet in our dreams can be anyone. They can be strangers. They can be benign. They can be evil. They can be saints, sinners, 1950s gas jockeys, or Phyllis Diller. Sometimes they speak. Sometimes they're silent. Sometimes, they're ill-tempered little men chasing you in black capes, lined in red.

We're moving now from the world of objects to that of sentient beings. Some characters in your dream may not be human. They may be cats, dogs, donkeys, or pangolins. They may speak to you in your language, or they may not.

The laws of the material world don't apply in the dreamscape. Of course, that's much of its attraction. There's nothing more appealing than to take advantage of a short, informative, healing, or even wild, chaotic departure from reality.

So, let's find out more about dream characters and the encounters we have with them. How we can enjoy them, and finally, how we can manifest/create or modify them to reflect a personal preference or agenda (as I did with Mr. "Get Off My Lawn").

Who Are These People?

Stephen LaBerge and Paul Tholey were some of the first to explore the meaning of the characters we encounter in lucid dreams and the interaction of dreamers with them.

While Tholey ascribed no spiritual significance to these characters, he did note they seemed to exist in the dreamer's mind as entities in their own right, featuring thought and action independent of the dreamer, at least on the conscious level.

For millennia, dream characters were considered real by dreamers. They were thought to be bearers of secrets and prognostication, having come to warn the dreamer of danger or even joyful impending life events or conditions. To the ancients, these characters were considered visitors from the spirit world.

But Freud posited that these characters were breakaway personality complexes generated by the dreamer's subconscious or subordinate personalities of the dreamer. Some believe these subordinate personalities (in a model similar to multiple personality syndrome) can control the dreamer's cognition and even physical movements in certain instances – fugue states, for example, where the person with these characters cropping up in certain instances dreams loses touch with reality.

But there has been no scientific evidence presented to support Freud's assertion, so, for the purposes of this book, feel free to attach whatever meaning of dreaming characters you please. There is no right answer here, as there is no empirical framework.

The people/characters we encounter in our dreams can be interacted with if you so choose. Dreamers can ask them questions to discover more about them – like what the heck they're doing in their dreams!

One way of conceptualizing characters in your lucid dreams is to realize they're most likely presenting from the same part of our psyches as whoever we're talking to in our internal dialogues. Sure, we're talking to ourselves – something I do all the time. But we're talking to an aspect of ourselves that inhabits a separate area of our consciousness. It's "us/not us." Our internal sounding board is where we bounce life off ourselves. We may rant, we may question, and we may struggle. But that inner sounding board is not very different from the characters we meet in our lucid dreams.

But Tholey and LaBerge discovered these characters would often surprise us when we question them in our lucid dreams. In one instance, a participant in one of the studies the two researchers conducted demanded that a dream character say a word with which the dreamer was unfamiliar. The dream character responded with the word, "orlog" – which was unknown to the dreamer. Interestingly, this Dutch word means "quarrel" or "squabble," and the lucid dream context the character appeared in bore precisely that emotional setting.

Tholey and LaBerge also observed that some dream characters would present information either foreign to or repugnant to the dreamer. Again, this points to a reality beyond Freud's theory of sub-personalities of the dreamer being generated by the subconscious, then arising in dreams. So, what might be a plausible explanation?

It might be (but this is by no means proven that these characters are a manifestation of Jung's collective unconscious) connecting us to thousands of years of human history and to countless billions who've walked the earth before us or who share it with us now. Are lucid dreams a means of communicating with the great ocean of knowledge stored just below the level of consciousness?

Perhaps, but absent reliable, empirical evidence, the phenomenon of dream characters remains a mystery.

So, how do we get to know these mysterious "beings"? How do we interact with them? Let's explore!

Stranger, new, or old friend (or a less pleasant visitor)?

The appearance or manifestation/spawn/creation of a dream character is always an opportunity. Whether benevolent or malevolent, there is an opportunity in every dream character you meet in your lucid dreams, whether you recognize the character or not.

Every character you meet in a lucid dream isn't a stranger. You'll recognize pets long departed from this earth, and other departed entities or representations of them. And if you're ready for doing so, you can manifest these people in lucid dreaming. Let's say you've already dreamed of a pet, family member, or friend you once knew. In that case, a manifestation is an idea that can help you achieve closure, the lack thereof being indicated by prior dream experiences.

And when you manifest characters personally known to you in a lucid dream, you work from a much more concrete idea. There is no ambiguity concerning the person or beloved pet you're trying to manifest. The ability to do this is a steppingstone to the manifestations of characters you don't know. But here is where you must be careful with your thoughts. The brain is a complex structure, and the connections it makes between our thoughts and the visuals connected to them can readily appear in our lucid dreams. That is not always a good thing.

So, before we go any further, we must explore the possibility of unfriendly or even hostile dream characters for a moment.

An article by Tadas Stumbrys of Vilnius University - Inner ghosts: Encounters with threatening dream characters in lucid dreams - presents an interesting theory about how best to deal with these less-than-ideal visitors.

In a German study, lucid dreamers reported that about 1/5th of dream characters they'd encountered were hostile. In these interactions, the lucid dreamers avoided the conflict by fighting, flying to escape, or resolving whatever the conflict was about. (The last strategy was more likely to be practiced by frequent lucid dreamers.)

Stumbrys concludes that other findings in the study indicate that hostile or threatening characters in lucid dreams may manifest because of the conflict in the dreamer's life or a mental health condition – or both. He suggests that choosing conflict resolution when encountering these unhappy campers is to wage peace by resolving the conflict. In that resolution is, Stumbrys suggests, healing on the psychological level, also.

While Stumbrys' commentary follows the Freudian interpretation of dream characters (psychic projections from the dreamer's subconscious mind), it should be remembered that nobody can yet explain dream characters scientifically. It's also helpful to know that healing old wounds is accessible to us all in lucid dreaming. When we confront ourselves and our lives in dreams, we're enjoying a highly individual experience available to no one else on earth, save through the medium of storytelling. But even then, the experience cannot truly be shared.

In lucidity, we enter the deepest level of ourselves, and that is incentive enough to grant ourselves the grace of healing. There is more to this art form than personal gain through self-improvement. Lucid dreaming is a tremendous opportunity to find the bleeding edges within us and sear them. When we bleed, we are weak. Wholeness and a sense of comfort in one's own skin are goals we can set aside our philosophical differences to attain. And in the end, the information serves to inform the practice, enriching it and basing it on a solid footing that we can all readily understand.

Hostility is a challenge that comes from the bleeding edges of the people modeling it. And so, in the hostile or threatening dream character, we meet a fellow traveler. That traveler has something to tell you. The hostility and sense of threat are intended to get your attention so that you'll address the message and respond to it.

Whatever that means to you, be honest with yourself as part of your ludic dreaming prep. What's lurking around in the back of your mind? You know it's not paying rent, whatever it is, so it's time to pack it up and ship it out.

Again, as I said above about manifesting the dream characters who represent people we know, the best way to deal with hostile characters at the beginning is choosing one of either fight or flight. Beginners will find flight far easier of the two, as they may not yet have developed enough confidence in the agility and strength (which are unlimited) of their dream body). You are the dreamer, and the body is yours, but to fight your way out of a hostile encounter requires supreme confidence. This is a much more advanced technique, requiring focus on the sensations of muscles engaging, the tension propelling the fight, and the hostile character behind the whole affair, all simultaneously.

My advice? Fly first, fight later.

As far as resolving the conflict is concerned, I hope that everyone reading will one day get to that level of lucid dreaming, as I believe there's an unspoken hope in conflict resolution at this highly personal level. If Freud was right, encounters with our intra-personal hostilities could only be a way toward a less stressful, conflicted life, which has a decided ripple effect. But if, in your explorations, you find that the theory holds up, then benefit. As we've already discussed, you make the rules in your dreamscape.

At this point, we're ready to hear from Jung's archetypes again but from the archetypes which guide human nature. As you launch your lucid dreaming journey, you'll recognize these archetypes. They attach to people you know, living and dead. They also manifest as our mysterious, unknown visitors. These 12 Jungian archetypes are crucial to understanding lucid dream characters and their roles in our dreams. What they represent is the storehouse of cultural knowledge in all the generations of humanity. Known to all of us, they are icons of our subconscious self-knowledge.

12 Archetypes

Ruler

The Ruler doesn't just love power. It's the ruler's reason for living, and power is maintained through the favored methodology of the ruler – control. While that sounds downright unattractive, the Ruler's goal is noble – prosperity for the family and the community! Rulers are responsible, taking care of business.

But Rulers are also heavy-handed, adhering to the motto "If you want anything done right, you need to do it yourself." There's that control issue again.

Rulers are Kings and Queens (not only monarchs but also within social structures and organizations), bosses, leaders, self-identified aristocrats, cocky politicians, managers, role models, and paper pushers. Rulers appear in all contexts, and you'll know one when you see one.

Look for the withering gaze and the upturned nose – the Ruler is routinely an egomaniac. Then again, the Ruler may appear in a dream to teach you something you need to know about your own sense of responsibility and control.

Creator/Artist

The Creator/Artist knows with certainty that whatever you can dream, you can do. Their greatest hope is that their creations will endure and find the audiences they were created for.

Creator/Visionaries detest mediocrity with a passion and won't tolerate it in themselves. Ever seeking perfection, the Creator/Visionary can get in her own way. Look for the unkempt, the distracted, and the vague.

This character comes to you as an emissary of your own creative potential, even to solve a problem in your life that's been worrying you.

The Sage

The sage's purpose in life is to unearth the truth, for nothing else will set humanity free. Obsessed with providing empirical proofs for reality, the Sage is finely analytical, rejecting the very suggestion that anyone could ever pull the wool over their learned eyes.

Living to understand at the deepest level, the Sage can get bogged down in details that block action.

Look for a child, the elderly, your high school math teacher, or a Medicine Man. In whatever form the Sage comes to your lucid dream, you will learn something of value.

The Innocent

While the word "innocence" has a deeply romantic connotation in contemporary society, it has an emotionally numbed, complacent, submissive quality to it in terms of this archetype.

The Innocent is languidly accepting, allowing life to wash over his malleable form. While their optimism speaks well of them and their faith in the universe rather noble, Innocents are primarily a bore, offering no play of emotional tension to break the pleasant monotony of their emotional landscape.

The Innocent may appear to you in the form of anyone but primarily those you know. Many of us know the Innocent and the complete lack of interest in reality modeled by this archetype. The Innocent may be your older brother, still living in your parents' basement, not yet knowing that the house has been sold. It could be a friend living on her credit cards while spending twice her monthly salary. This archetype is characterized by its almost boneless properties and its tedium.

The Explorer

Dashing and fearless, The Explorer is ready for anything as she travels the world. Through exploring the physical world, The Explorer reaches toward himself and the truth about who she is.

Focused on authenticity and fulfillment, The Explorer shies from conformity. The demands of polite society are like shackles to this archetype, as The Explorer is the archetype of immediacy and freedom.

The Explorer comes to visit to remind you of your most cherished dreams, fulfilling your bucket list, and your hopes for your children. The Explorer may be a trusted figure from your past or present, a friend or relative. The Explorer may be a stranger with a message of realizing the joy of freedom by discovering our authenticity in the immediacy and urgency of life.

The Rebel

Buckle up, Buttercup, if you're getting a visit from The Rebel. This archetype is ready to rumble. The Rebel never saw a rule he didn't want to break or a revolution he didn't want to be part of.

And don't tick him off, or he may grant you a little dream character hostility with that attitude of hers. The Rebel has no time for trivialities. There are systems to kick over and reboot.

A visit from this wild man means it's time to shake things up. You know that on some level, but this badass visiting a lucid dream means that you do, too. The Rebel calls you to bold, life-changing action.

The Hero

The Hero is an irrepressible warrior, standing for the triumph of valor over cowardice. Like the Black Knight in the film "Monty Python's Holy Grail," losing a leg is but a flesh wound to the stubborn, conflict-prone Hero archetype.

With a chip on his shoulder a mile high, The Hero lives to demonstrate his prowess and fearlessness, believing this is how the world will be saved. It's easy to see why The Hero is such an important archetype, encompassing both a type of garden variety, low-level narcissism, and a noble desire to fight for what's right. In truth, most of us aspire to heroism of some kind.

The Hero appears in your lucid dream to prod you forward when you feel you're unable or unequipped, reminding you to be the best you can be. The Hero doesn't buy your excuses.

As much as the Hero may be Monty Python's stubborn Black Knight, he's also the loud, obnoxious drill sergeant in Full Metal Jacket. When you feel like quitting, The Hero will be getting in your face if you're not watering the garden of your goals.

The Magician

You may have noticed that the 12 Archetypes are like all people – a blend of good and bad, positive and negative. The Magician, of course, is the same. Believing in her own power to construct the reality around her, The Magician's purpose is to realize her fondest dreams without getting into hot water.

That's where the manipulation – the true magic – happens. The Magician's seductive power can be put to the wrong uses, just as our own can be. All the same, The Magician is also a healer and Shaman, bringing balm to Gilead when there is none to be had.

The Magician's visit can mean many things, one of them that you're in need of healing – whether physically or psychologically. This is rarely a casual visit. Pay close attention to the contents of dreams involving this archetype.

The Jester

If one thing may be said of The Jester, it's that he keeps you laughing. The Jester is here for the party – every party! A madcap and all-around bon vivant, The Jester can't stand the serious side of life. It's all just a big, crazy joke.

While the Jester is scads of silly fun, The Jester can also be a bit of a pain, getting in the way of getting anything done. Youthful and with no concept of passing time, life is to be lived, to The Jester doesn't slow down to pay annoying bills or show up for boring work after a tear-away night on the town.

The Jester showing up either means you need to get more fun into your life or that you need some of the fun if your life to take a step back. Either way, the visitor can take on any appearance you or he chooses, so be sure to make a conscious decision about the Jester's appearance if you're afraid of clowns. But just so you're aware – if that's the case, The Jester will most likely choose precisely that appearance, so be prepared. Not all jokes are funny.

Every Man/Woman

What this archetype wants – more than anything else in the world – is to be like everyone else. With a strong belief in the fundamental equality of all humans, the Everyman/woman settles for mediocrity because mediocrity is what most people settle for.

This Archetype is a joiner, connecting with others in every way possible in the community. Desiring belonging, every man/woman lives in terror of standing out or not being included.

But The Everyman/woman is empathic and down to earth, embodying familiar values that most of us hold fast to, whether we live them out or not. And that's what The Everyman/woman comes to red flag for you. Are you settling for second best out of a desire to belong? Not leaving a job you're dissatisfied with because you're friends with everyone there? Or do you feel alienated by over-achievement? Everyman/woman might be appearing in your lucid dream to remind you of where you came from, Jenny from the Block, or maybe, to remind you of where you should be.

The Lover

While it's true that love makes the world go around, a surfeit of love can make The Lover disappear into the needs of those around him, so intense is the love this archetype is infused with.

Love is all you need in the world of The Lover. It's what makes The Lover's heartbeat and his only reason for being. The primary need of this archetype is love, with its intimacy and sensuality.

When The Lover comes to you, whether in the form of Jake Gyllenhaal or a bridge troll, the message is clear. Love is coming; love is leaving – it's either love longed for or lamented. The extravagant warmth of this archetype comes to make way for love, to heal the wounds of love, or to clarify your unstated longing for love.

The Caregiver

The Caregiver archetype represents the mission, unconditional love, and service. Like The Lover, the caregiver is vulnerable to disappearing into the needs of others. But with the caregiver, this amounts to conscious martyrdom. This speaks to the caregiver's selfishness and the unbalanced nature of those who feed the needs of others without giving themselves sufficient self-care.

Most of us like to help others, but we damage our ongoing ability to continue when we neglect ourselves to extend that help. The caregiver may be visiting your dreams to share that reality with if you're overextended. But the caregiver may also be appearing for the sake of encouraging you to do the volunteer work you keep putting off.

Dream characters can certainly be spawned, manifested, or created by lucid dreamers. And who you meet in your lucid dreams becomes much more under your control the more you develop your skills in the dream space. This is especially true of dream characters. When you're confident about your own role in the dream and your motivations in any given dream scenario, you're much more likely to benefit from the lessons dream characters – especially the Jungian archetypes – come to you to share.

Chapter Nine: Exploring Your Dreamscape and Top 10 Things to Do

Now that we've explored objects and dream characters, it's time to slow down and take in the scenery. And that scenery might be *anything!* It can be what your mind subconsciously assembles, or it can be what you choose. It can be a combination of what those two origins create when they collide in your lucid dreaming state of consciousness.

In this chapter, we'll talk about where you'll be in the dreamscape and the top 10 things you can do while you're there.

The Lay of the Land

Your dream landscape can consist of anything from your local shopping mall to bring in your old senior high school to a farmer's field to a mountaintop. What you see in a dreamscape is up to you and your subconscious mind. Even when lucid dreaming, there are elements of all dreams which may appear spontaneously. Of course, the advantage of lucid dreaming is that the details may be amended at will, depending on your preferences.

Much depends on your frame of mind as you enter the lucid dream. What matters to you at that moment? What's on your mind, and what are your current goals in life? What brings you joy? Do you feel optimistic?

Your frame of mind and how you navigate that factor is one of the most crucial elements of lucid dreaming if you're seeking to benefit from your dreams. Whether the benefit you seek is psychological healing, ongoing peace and equanimity, or related to your station in life, your frame of mind is important to your success in the art of lucid dreaming. And you have much to do with that.

We all tend to blame our moods on external circumstances, but the truth is that we choose how we respond to the vagaries of life. We can play the victim or project ourselves toward the transcendence of life's curveballs and pitfalls. Lucid dreaming can help you with that. It will teach you that the dream itself is the thing that matters. Just as your state of mind determines how you'll emerge from difficult life circumstances, lucid dreams and your ability to be their architect will support you in finding the way forward. It's just another tool to use in life and a powerful one that can help you understand how to reach that pleasant state of knowing you are the one you've been waiting for.

In the world of lucid dreaming, the lay of the land is your playground. You are the architect of the set (dreamscape), the director - and the casting director!

Let's review a few of the physical elements you may encounter in the dreamscape to start you seeing what significance they may have to you personally – and their global meanings, as well.

Mountains

Mountains have a long and glorious history in symbolism, both waking and sleeping. Martin Luther King Jr. drew on the biblical narrative of Moses looking down at the Promised Land from a mountaintop but never being permitted to enter the land he'd led his people to. In the last speech he ever gave in his life, delivered in Memphis on the night before he was gunned down on the balcony of the Loraine Hotel by James Earl Ray, he says, "I may not get there with you." And he didn't. But his work led to tremendous change. And while the Promised Land is still a mirage for many, today, Dr. King's visionary work pushed the agenda of freedom further toward realization.

And mountaintop visions are momentous when they are part of a dreamscape. They appear to remind you to hold on to what matters to you. Are you, for example, attempting to scale a figurative Everest to prove something to other people? If that's the case, the effort isn't serving you. It's undermining you and draining your energy for the sake of appeasing others and what they have to say about the success of your efforts.

Cold, snowy mountains are an indication of prosperous, peaceful times and of impending change. Change is feared by many, but ice and snow on your mountain landscape mean that change is to be embraced, not feared or resisted. Change is inevitable and as reliable as the mountains themselves.

If, while in the mountains, you come upon an alpine meadow, expansive and dotted with wildflowers, a part of you is longing to be free. If you're staying in a job or a relationship or any other life circumstance that feels safe but not satisfying, you're on the cusp of change but hanging tight for comfort. A dream of open spaces in a mountain setting calls for you to stop hesitating and level up.

Hills

Rolling hills are a symbol of the unknown. What's concealed in their hidden gorges and valleys is a source of anxiety for some dreamers because what's unknown is often feared in waking reality and in dreams. Gullies and such are dark places we'd rather not explore.

It's how you interact with the landscape that's important, in the instance of rolling hills. Do you gaze at them with wonder, imagining all the wonderful secrets you'll find in their gullies? Or do you take a long way around to avoid those hidden crevices that lurk between those mysterious hills?

The unknown is scary to most of us. It's beyond our human capacity to control, and so, we prefer to avoid uncertainty and ambiguity at all costs. We choose safety over exploration, and this causes our souls significant atrophy. When hills appear in your dream, ask yourself if those hills might not be calling you to a step in your soul's development, and then explore blissfully!

A Garden

A garden may be a question, an answer, or a symbol. As a question, a garden appearing in your dreamscape is asking you if it isn't time to nurture a part of yourself you've been neglecting. Just as the beautiful garden has appeared, so might that part of yourself, once it's been properly watered.

The garden also appears as an answer to our deepest, unresolved questions. These questions usually revolve around ontological (referring to the essence of our beings) issues, like sexuality, vocation (springing from our gifts and aptitudes), or purpose (what our gifts and aptitudes have been formed to do). The garden can also be about the question of marriage and children. If you're not sure, the garden may hold a specific answer. That answer may take the form of a flower, plant, or bird. You may be addressed by a dream character, asking another question. But the garden asks you the questions you need to answer to be who you were born to be.

The garden is also a semiotic message. A healthy, vibrant garden is about prosperity and growth, but it's also a symbol of the impermanence of all living things. The message is always tailored to the individual in a lucid dream and subject to the manipulation of the dreamer, but the universal semiotic is growth, new life, and life's eternal cycles.

A dying garden can symbolize either the obvious - death, decay, rot, or, like the healthy garden, life's eternal cycle. The dying or dead garden may also be a sign of change - for better or for worse.

Now that you've had a taste of some classical landscape features that show up in our dreams -lucid and otherwise - symbolize, let's move on to your role as the architect of your dreamscape.

Spawning the Dreamscape

In the chapters on dream objects and dream characters, we discussed that spawning/creating/manifesting is your ability to concentrate on the effort of producing the dream element you're going for while not concentrating so hard that the quality of your lucid dream degrades or collapses.

For that purpose, not biting off more than you chew is a stabilizing thought to remember. As we've discussed in the chapters just mentioned, sticking to what you know best and can visualize most readily is how you build your ability to manifest.

We build from what we already know. The information we have in our minds about any given topic forms the foundation of all our skills. It's the same with lucid dreaming. What you're familiar with is your cognitive link to the goal - improving your ability to spawn your dream features and direct the action.

With dreamscapes, you might start by transforming certain elements (adding trees, plants, animals, etc.). If you're not ready for the unknown represented by rolling hills, for example, you might substitute them for a river meandering through a valley. Or you might prefer to be in an alpine meadow, flying to nearby mountains. But the trick is to focus on an element you feel you can effectively and almost effortlessly visualize into the dreamscape.

Starting from a real-world example, your dreamscapes needn't make real-world sense. For example, you might decide you'd like the Roman Coliseum in your alpine meadow. It's your dream. You build it with the available skills to your personal vision.

A garden in your world - possibly your own - might be your dreamscape. If the garden is yours and you are the gardener, then this is the ideal dreamscape, as you've planted everything in it yourself, with care. In the dreamscape, you know the garden so well that you can manipulate it at will. A garden you know intimately is also a great setting for spawning objects and even characters. When you know the garden, you know where you want things to appear, so you already have at your disposal a splendid template for your lucid dreaming efforts.

Favorite places, vacation memories, impressions that have remained in your mind your whole life - all these are excellent fodder to get you started with manifesting dream landscapes. What you are most familiar with, what you know in the finest detail, is a tremendous tool for lucid dreaming. It creates an outpost of your world in the land of dreams and a solid foundation for building your creative skills in that environment.

Now, let's talk about the *Top 10 Things to Do* in your dreamscape. These are just to get you started, as I'm sure you'll have plenty of your own ideas. We will talk about some interesting ways to experience the dreamscape!

1. Talk to Heroes, Villains, and Dead Relatives

Lucid dreaming is not a séance, but we all have our heroes, and who wouldn't love to meet them? As for villains, wouldn't you love to dress down some of the globe's more unsavory characters, past and present, possibly blow them up or drop 16 tons on their heads? Hey, it's your dream! And if you feel the need, the lucid dream space is a safe place to vent.

As for dead relatives, your grandmother may have left the world without passing on her world-famous divinity fudge recipe. A skilled dreamer might not be able to get the whole recipe, but wouldn't a dream visitation trigger some memories that could help? And even if it didn't, you'd be having a chat with your gran, wouldn't you?

If you're planning on attempting to spawn a hero (anyone from Elizabeth I to General Patton), then prepare yourself by reacquainting yourself with the appearance of the personality you're spawning. If your hero is contemporary, hearing them speak can give your knowledge greater texture. The more of that there is, the more likely you'll succeed.

2. Go on an International Jaunt

Have you always longed to see the Great Wall of China? The Pyramids? All this and more is possible in the lucid dreamscape. As I've said above, regarding heroes, gather the most detailed knowledge you can about the place you'd like to visit in your dreams. Video, photographs, and articles that describe the destination's ambiance provide multiple references in your mind, so it can connect the dots to manifest it.

Getting there is much easier (and cheaper) than it is in real life. Spinning (see Chapter 5) is an excellent way to achieve this. The facsimile of physical movement reboots the circuits of your lucid dreaming. If you intend to be at the destination of your choice, spinning will get you there.

3. Time Travel

You may want to revisit your favorite childhood Christmas or another cherished memory from your life. But time travel in lucid dreams needn't be limited to our personal experiences.

Projecting your dream self into a defunct reality is an action requiring significant knowledge of the period you're targeting, which encompasses events of the time, common dress and speech, customs, architecture, and social constructs. Time travel is complex, and while you may experience it, it's an advanced activity that's quite demanding. Enthusiasts of certain historical periods will have the most luck with this adventure. But it's possible for those willing to spend the time preparing. That preparation includes looking at images from the period you'd like to visit before bed as part of your chosen preparation for the night's dreaming.

4. Practice Living Out Your Dreams

You have serious designs on the future, but you're not there yet. Maybe your goal is to win an Academy Award or give an acceptance speech the night of your huge election win. Or maybe you want to learn to dance Flamenco or sing in front of an audience.

Dreaming is free, and whatever your ambitions entail, lucid dreaming is a great way to try your life goals and dreams on for size. If you're interested in lucid dreaming, then I'm sure you have some experience with visualization, readers. And lucid dreaming is like a live-action adjunct to visualization in which you direct the action. While you can say the same about visualization, the form of consciousness employed isn't the same. Nor is waking consciousness as profound as lucid dreaming.

The profundity of lucid dreaming is in its proximity to the work of your subconscious. Lucid dreaming grants you contact with your subconscious dynamically. In lucid dreams, you actively enlist it in the work you're doing in your life. The visualization becomes an immediate, although temporal and illusory, reality.

5. Learn a Skill

Again, visualization pales in comparison to the lucid dream state of consciousness. Preparation for this activity entails discovering more about the skill you want to learn.

You may have been fascinated with embroidery your whole life or carpentry and have never learned. Why not start learning in the lucid dream space? Visualization posits that what you can imagine yourself doing, you can eventually do. Lucid dreaming is an even more profound experience of that effect.

Say you'd like to learn how to play the flute. Prepare by listening to masters of the instrument, intensely focusing on the specific sound of the flute. Then visualize yourself playing it, mimicking the movements of the hands and use of breath. Know what shape your mouth should take to propel your breath through the instrument.

In lucid dreams, the sound is more intense. Music, especially, takes on an almost material presence. So, as you dream, discover a new skill and carry the experience over into the waking world. If you can get lucid dream it, you can do it.

6. Talk to Animals

These days, many people who'd love to have pets are not permitted to because of onerous regulations imposed by landlords and Homeowners Associations. But your lucid dreams don't have those characters (unless you want them to), so you aren't bound by rules.

And the animals you spawn in your dreams can be anything from a fluffy kitty to a Chihuahua to a Siberian tiger (take care with that one).

Domestic animals that you have abundant experience with are best for this purpose. You know them, and their behavior is relatively predictable. So, start with a pet, you know - maybe one from your childhood or a beloved pet who has crossed the Rainbow Bridge. What would your pet say to you? What would you say to your pet?

Maybe all you want is a quiet cuddle session with a dearly departed pet you miss. But maybe you want to interact with wild birds or coyotes. Whatever you desire, manifest the animal or animals by focusing on their specific characteristics in preparation and then resolve to visit with them in your lucid dreams.

7. Solve Problems

The lucid dream space offers many opportunities to find solutions to problems in your waking life. Asking the right questions is important here.

For example, if you find yourself in a job or a relationship that's making you unhappy or has you feeling stuck, the dream space is where you have the freedom to get to the root of the problem.

You might even want to manifest a version of yourself to talk to in the dream. Often, we push troublesome thoughts to the back of our minds as we carry on with our lives. That can cost us, as the problem doesn't go away. It festers in the darkness of our minds, where it can morph into unpleasant thoughts and the behaviors that arise from them, making matters worse.

Getting to the root of the problem means being honest with yourself about your hopes, dreams, and needs. Sometimes the only place to do that kind of work is in the non-judgmental dreamscape. Others can't judge us here. We can't even judge ourselves. We can only seek the information that might serve as a catalyst for our positive action.

8. Get Intimate

Sex in the age of COVID19 is no laughing matter, especially for singles. But COVID19 isn't the only communicable illness we have to prepare ourselves for encountering in the waking world. So, the lucid dream space provides us with a safe place to live out our sexualities.

You may be questioning your sexuality. What better place for actively questioning it could there be than a lucid dream? And because you're in charge, you can create the partner you want to even the minutest detail.

The fact you're in control means you drive the action. The manifestation of your dream partner will not spontaneously initiate. That's your job! Go in there with confidence, knowing that you're the architect and the director, and enjoy some guilt-free sex without fear of contracting an STD or getting pregnant! And remember that in the lucid dream space, it's always "just for fun."

9. Wander at Will

This feature of lucid dreaming will be especially attractive to women. It's often difficult for women to go where they want to go without fear of lurking predators. Women may appreciate a nightscape, for this reason, in their lucid dreams.

Imagine having the freedom to wander at will, enjoying the moonlight and sounds of the night all around, without fear or anxiety? The more detail you're able to envision before falling asleep, the greater your territory will be. And as you go, you'll discover another world. It might not exist in the waking world, but doesn't that make it even more beautiful? It's yours. The night is yours, and you are free to explore without fear.

10. Eat!

Have food allergies cramped your culinary style? Maybe you avoid certain foods because of celiac or lactose intolerance. Or maybe you feel as though you can't even look at food without gaining weight.

Lucid dreaming is the answer! I used to love shellfish, but I've developed an allergy to it in recent years that causes me to break out in hives. Nothing could be worse for a shellfish lover! But I can overeat on all the crawfish etouffee and lobster with drawn butter my crustacean-loving heart desires in my lucid dreams.

Don't just picture your favorite foods to prepare. Recall the scent, the taste, the presentation, and the texture of the food in your mouth. Remember as many details as you can before entering the lucid dream state. Then, enjoy whatever it is you've spawned to eat, without guilt and hives!

I hope you'll be able to get started on creating your own lucid dream landscapes and activities from the information offered in this chapter. Next, we'll explore the realm of spirit guides and how you can work with them to unlock a deeper experience of lucid dreaming.

Chapter Ten: Working with Your Spirit Guides

Before we dive in, I think it's important for readers to understand at least a little about the concept of spirit guides and from where this concept originally sprang.

While prominent in Western Spiritualist circles, spirit guides didn't arise from the "West" as we now think of it. Spirit guides arose from African pre-colonialist societies and the spirituality found in them.

Little research has been conducted into African pre-colonialist spirituality, but like most indigenous spiritual practices, there is an emphasis on the spirits of ancestors guiding the lives of the living. Unlike the culturally appropriated model of spirit guides in the West, there is no appeal to angels or archangels (which came with Christianity, colonialism's standard-bearing Faith system). The ball is firmly in the court of the ancestors, believed to be akin to a kind of "living dead" among those genuinely living. This may sound like the zombie apocalypse, but the idea of the dead living among us has nothing to do with that. Rather, spirit guides are active presences, supporting and guiding those they communicate with to create better outcomes in their lives by applying the ancient wisdom they carry with them.

In 2016, Dalian and Verona Spence-Adofo published the results of 7 years of research into African spirituality, entitled Ancestral Voices: Spirit is Eternal. They discovered in their research that there are six key pillars of African spirituality, namely:

- Existence and its nature
- Balance and order in existence
- That all is interconnected and interdependent
- The hierarchy of spirit and society
- The cycles of life
- The spirit inherent in living

All that exists in African spirituality – whether animate or inanimate – is considered within the Divine (panentheism – that all things are in God). African spirituality has no canon (written Holy Books), being passed down through generations in the form of songs, spoken word, and life lessons, from healing plants and spiritual healing to rites of passage and communal behaviors.

The spirit guides of African spirituality are believed to live in homes we can't see, communicating with the living from this distant place that exists parallel to the material world. There is also a belief (shared in the three major monotheistic faiths – Judaism, Christianity, and Islam) that what happens in the material order impacts the spiritual parallel and vice versa.

In common with other indigenous belief systems, humanity interacts with its environment as part of a symbiotic relationship, encompassing tradition and culture. The totality of life is recognized as that encompassing those who passed over to the other side of it in the ancestors. The ancestors are considered divinely mandated deities (but perhaps in a less autocratic sense that deities are conceptualized in the West).

Voodoo, which has a rather strange and sensationalistic reputation in the West, features a system of spirit guides (ancestor-deities) who descend directly from pre-colonialist African spirituality and its own system of spirit guides. In Voodoo, spirit guides both advise practitioners and intervene in human affairs when summoned by a specific community. The syncretism (blending of beliefs) which occurred between African spirituality and the colonialist Church in Africa rendered the saints of the Catholic Church as "loa" blended into the existing pantheon of ancestor-deities (double-represented usually). Eventually, it became the practice of Voodoo in colonies with a large African presence due to the Atlantic slave trade. The syncretic introduction of the saints into the belief system of Africans kidnapped from their homeland was practiced in appeasement of slave owners, who demanded that their "property" become Christian. And so, what was accomplished was a veil over traditional African spirituality, which allowed for its continuing practice in the colonies, especially but not limited to Haiti.

This brief and admittedly scanty history of spirit guides is necessary for a fuller understanding when we enter a discussion about them, their role, and their purpose. This is Holy ground we're about to tread on, and I ask that readers consider their approach, which must be one of great respect.

Approaching Your Spirit Guides

If you've ever asked St. Anthony to help you find something that was lost - like your keys - then you know exactly what you need to do.

The spirit guides exist in the realm beyond the material world and are always present. What they are not is autocratic. They respect your boundaries and will not attend unless their presence is specifically requested.

Remember, though; spirit guides are not St. Anthony. Neither are spirit guides stand-ins for the tooth fairy or the mythical "genie in a bottle." They're not part of the universe for the sake of leaving a dime under your pillow.

Spirit guides are not to be invoked over petty matters. They are there to guide and support your life decisions. Maintain some perspective when calling on the spirit guides and remember what I've said above: approach with respect.

Spirit guides would not be able to guide us had they not known at least one earthly incarnation. This reality provides perspective on the material world, its challenges, and its pleasures. The disembodied, in other words, have not always been so. While the indigenous model of ancestral connection and communion is certainly about the experience of incarnation joining the spiritual and material realms together, it's also about the sense of ambiguity, especially around the loa, in Voodoo. In our model, which echoes African spirituality at its root, these two senses operate together. The ancestors are with us, but so are those who represent the same guiding principles as the loa of Voodoo, many of whom predate colonialism.

While the saints of Catholicism are to be prayed to, the loa are there to serve the living. In so doing, they fulfill a vital role as a link to the Creator, who everything and everyone in both the spiritual and material realms serves.

Before we move into meeting your spirit guides (there are usually several - a kind of spiritual posse), I'd like to describe one of the most important loa in Haitian vodun, for the sake of drawing a parallel to your own spirit guides. (NB: You may know some instinctively and sometimes, remember them from your earlier life or even from photographs. But you will not recognize your spirit guides by sight. You will recognize them by way of a much more profound connection.)

So, let's describe one of the better-known loa, Erzulie Freda, loa of love. Freda is part of the Erzulie family of loa. This group of loa is associated with water (fluidity, change through persistence over time).

Also known as "Lady Erzulie," Freda is flirtatious, disappointing lovers as a way of life, and those she "rides" (spiritual possession in the trance state). But Freda is also associated with Our Lady of Sorrows of the Catholic Church (there's that syncretism thing). Our Lady of Sorrows is a saint of the Church representing Mary as the suffering mother of the Crucified Christ. So, there is more to Erzulie Freda than being a relentless flirt and fickle lover. She is also the mother who suffers.

The complexity of this loa indicates how much more there is to the loa system of Voudon than public perception gives it credit for. The same may be said of spirit guides in the context of the West and the pursuit of lucid dreaming – it's complicated!

That's why I wanted to provide some historical perspective concerning the way spiritualism in the West has drawn on other cultural realities to find a solution for its apparent spiritual restlessness. Because of the ancient basis of a belief in spirit guides (which throwback to pre-history), these details are more important to understand than you might think.

The truth is that as you explore spirit guides and which your own might be, you're connecting to a human tradition that has existed for countless generations. Common among all indigenous people before the incursion of colonialism, it may serve to remember that we were all indigenous to some point on the compass back in the mists of time. These traditions, then, are human legacy. But they are a human legacy that the European West has disconnected from, having chosen other spiritual frameworks to supplant those of the ancients. And here, we're reconnecting to that ancient font of spiritual succor – our ancestors and the spirits of wisdom.

Connecting

Your spirit guides have always been with you. They have always known and cared about you.

These disembodied entities have experienced human life before. They are your ancestors, but they may have only been your ancestors briefly, as spirit guides are eternal entities that pass through many earthly incarnations.

When we talk to ourselves or reflect on problems or challenges, we remember the past lessons. We remember the things wise people around us have advised. We return to the lesson in our minds. This internalized dialogue with the past is part of what the spirit guide is. They not only know you intimately, they know the world in the same deep and detailed way, only much more potently and fully.

We hear the voices in our heads of those who guided us in our lives in times of challenge. We seek their advice. With spirit guides, we do the same. But sometimes, the spirit guides who accompany us in our lives reach out first.

This has happened to me on two occasions. On the first of these, I was a child. As the older of two siblings, I was assigned the private enclave of a large, downstairs room. One night, I woke up (at least I believe I did - I now believe I was lucid dreaming). I saw a woman standing in the doorway of my room, wearing a summer dress printed with abstract flowers, a straw hat, and sunglasses.

Immediately, I put my head under the covers and began screaming for my parents. I had no idea who this mysterious woman was or why she was standing in the doorway of my room. She was the first visit I was to experience.

The second visit I can recall with any certainty is a dream I had as an adult. This was not a lucid dream but a conventional one. I was standing on the side of the street, at night, with cars driving by.

Suddenly, a Citroen car passed by, packed full of women. All the women seemed to be middle-aged and wore kerchiefs over their heads with long braids cascading from them. As they passed, they called to me and waved. They were smiling, displaying abundant gold teeth. When I woke up, I knew that I had seen my spirit guides.

These were the only spontaneous visitations I had. As I came to understand what spirit guides were and their role in helping me find my forward in life, I began to talk to them. As a writer, I talk to myself a lot (it goes with the territory), but I understand that it's not really me I'm talking to. The internal dialogues of the past are externalized to create a dialogue that inhabits both temporal spaces. With spirit guides, we have access to wisdom and knowledge that transcends that of the former dialogues with wise people we've encountered. The depth and breadth of what can be shared with us greatly increases.

Direct "outreach" by spirit guides is not as uncommon as you may think. If you're not accustomed to their presence (as I wasn't during my visitation by the woman in the snappy summer outfit), we may miss signs that contact is being attempted. There are several key indications this is what's happening.

- Increased frequency of vivid lucid dreams, including visitations. These dreams might feature visuals of your guides like the two I've experienced.
- Reception of symbolic articles – white feathers that suddenly appear near you or on you, lost keys found in unusual or unexpected places, other unusual articles appearing, some of which probably have special significance to you
- Intuition is sharpened. We arrive at conclusions about situations and people more quickly and confidently

- You may find yourself responding to music as though you'd never listened to it before. If so, immediately seek out the lyrics online to see if they might not lead you to answers to questions currently in your mind
- Repeatedly seeing a word, a phrase, or a number. This is an oblique attempt to answer the presenting question by other means
- The sudden feeling you need to do something or go somewhere you had given little importance to before. You may feel compelled to follow through without really understanding why. Spend time with the sensation to test it. If it persists, you are being reached out to

Inviting

Spirit guides only intervene in the affairs of their charges when visitation has become an urgent necessity in their wise opinion. When I was visited the first time, I was navigating a difficult stage of childhood in pre-adolescence. My guide reassured me but ended up frightening me. To this day, I can't be sure why, but I believe it was what the transition meant for a girl. Perhaps she'd felt it was an urgent need, as I wasn't prepared for what ensued once the day came and, suddenly, there it was.

Scary! Sorry I screamed at you, summer spirit guide! I needed you, and I didn't even know it. And that's the thing to remember about the role of spirit guides. They operate as a part of you that's beyond your reach. It's the knowledge you already have within you but don't want to know. They bring it to the surface so you can deploy it as a life skill.

On the second occasion, I was at a time in my life during which I was friends with a family I hadn't realized was deeply dysfunctional. The father, who I believed at the time was merely eccentric, was also autocratic and controlling. I started to see the man's eccentricities more as symptoms of something going very wrong in him. It was sinister.

Things got worse until the man's wife and cousin and the elderly woman who lived with them were dead by his hand. My guides had come to warn me. The Citroen they were riding in was the same as the one the violent husband drove - even the same color. I'll spare you the gruesome details, but I was lucky to live through that one, and I thank my gold-toothed, babushka-wearing spirit guides for that.

So, you see - times must be dire for them to come to you. But outreach on your part is a way of developing the relationship between you to benefit more fully on both your parts. Your outreach isn't something that happens every day in the world of the spirits - where far too many languished unfulfilled due to the contemporary West's spiritual malaise.

Inviting your spirit guides is the same as any type of prayer, affirmation, or mantra. The invitation is a powerful signal to your spirit guides that their purpose is recognized. This not only gives them a warm fuzzy but contributes to the spiritual journey they're dedicated to in their disembodied state.

An effective and respectful relationship with a spirit guide can only result from the same root as friendship: Genuine sympathy, genuine mutual interest, and just genuineness. A disingenuous approach will get you no place fast with the sophisticated spirit guide. They know what color cow droppings are.

Choose Your Framework Only When You Believe It

I hope you're getting excited about having a fresh look at spirit guides. As part of that, I would also like readers to consider that being confident about the framework you intend to approach your spirit guides from within is the only factor that will hold it up.

You are enjoined to believe in what you're attempting to do. For that reason, if you can't accept the idea of a disembodied reality that exists parallel to our own, so what? I believe that's secondary to seeking to connect with a part of yourself only they can reveal.

Cast them as psychobiological functions if that's what makes you feel comfortable. Nothing about lucid dreaming or the hope of meeting spirit guides is about believing in an ideology. Ideology is, in fact, the enemy of reason, requiring the suspension of critical thought in favor of a manifesto or a confessional.

Your mind is your own, and how you choose to apply it is yours alone – within reason.

So, whether a spirit guide from our psychobiological past or a disembodied phenomenon, spirit guides are readily available to you. They know what you don't and lead where you haven't been.

And surely, a walk through the subconscious demands a good guide. Take your pick and be rewarded, enriched, and greatly changed.

Chapter Eleven: Creating A Dream Sanctuary

"Dreaming, in any of its various forms, is life-changing, so if what you're looking for is your current life unchanged but with an easier cash flow and an end to all emotional upheaval, this isn't the way to find it."

Manda Scott

Because this chapter explains a methodology for creating a dream sanctuary, I think it's important that we understand the context of the idea, which is Shamanism.

Manda Scott is a writer in the United Kingdom with a keen interest in Shamanism and its practices. As she eloquently states, "Shamanic practice is the modern extension of indigenous spiritualities." As we've already discussed in the last chapter, spirit guides come from precisely the same source.

And I believe the point being made by Scott here is a salient one: that the West's interest in Shamanism doesn't necessarily equate to the profound truth of the original articulation. But as I've also pointed out, it's all our legacy to explore. And this, Scott, does mindfully as we all should seek to do.

So, let's discuss creating a dream sanctuary with a little more texture with the addition of some context about Shamanism and the role of the dream sanctuary in it.

Shamanism's 3 Pillars

Shamanic dreaming is threefold, encompassing conventional dreaming, lucid dreaming, and waking dreams (every day, fully functioning consciousness, as opposed to the state of lucidity).

This type of dreaming is part of a three-pillar structure in Shamanic practice. One of those accompanying dreaming is *ritual*. Ritual practice is the tangible, firmly grounded in the material world, using elements thereof. This roots the practitioner in reality, consecrating the immaterial with the sacred material as ordained by the Creator.

Ritual is based on the four directions related to the four points on the compass. This ties the directions and compass points to the four elements: earth, air, wind, and fire. The sensuality of Shamanic ritualism is repeated in recognizable ways throughout surviving indigenous cultures in the world. The material is sanctified in reciprocation by the immaterial, in an eternal cycle of renewal and mutuality. Without one, there is not the other in this spirituality. As body and spirit are one, so are tangible and intangible. There is no veil, no matter how flimsy. All is just one thing. And all are accessible.

There is no rigid way to express Shamanism ritually. It's the practitioner's decision, as it is in every religion, despite the iron claw of dogma.

The final pillar of Shamanism is, of course, Shamanic journeying - a central practice in Shamanism. Using the beat of a drum, the practitioner travels to reality's other levels, meeting with teachers, spirit guides, animals, teachers, and the resident deities.

Shamanism's essence is finding union with all that exists in all reality's hidden pockets, just as Buddhism's is. To become one is to conquer the perilous duality that plagues Western society, separating the human-animal and all others into categories that assign value. This is destructive, and Shamanism seeks to heal it. But in the West, there is no such thing as a Shaman.

Scott's contention is there is no such thing as a Shaman in Western society. That reason can be found in Shamanism's two central teachings:

- **How to Live**

Shamanism is committed to mindfulness and the need to live in each moment with appreciation and gratitude. This is how to live, not chasing money and all that pursuit entails. Rather, living is about being part of all that is an integral contributor.

- **How to Die**

Humility is the keyword here, replacing the West's obsession with reward and punishment. It's part of the package! By living in the world as it presents itself in each moment of our lives, we greet the transition of death with equanimity.

By approaching death with humility, we lose our cloying demand for certainty and assurances. There's no reward and no punishment. Death just is because, and we have no idea what that means. All our efforts to cast it as a threat to the living are in vain. All the posthumous paradises we're promised reflect our own craven desires and not any known truth. Humility is what gets us around our own grasping, dissatisfied egos.

These two reasons are the principle blockade to Shamans existing in a Western context. This society simply does not accommodate qualities like humility or mindfulness. Our minds are too focused on struggle and conquest, binaries and individuation to accommodate either and thus, not terribly Shaman-friendly.

The Role of the Dream Sanctuary

A dream sanctuary is a safe place where your spirit guides, your ancestors, and other dream characters, who appear in lucid dreams to work with you, can meet. This is a long-term building project, demanding patience and focus.

As you've read about manifesting objects, characters, and dreamscapes, now you can create a safe place for your dream advisors to confer with you about matters of urgency and importance in your spiritual, psychological, and waking life, in general.

What's important here is that the space is stable and feels safe. Manifesting the space successfully is rooted in detail. Your more detail in your mind about the dream sanctuary, the more stable and inviolable it will be. You might even think of it as a citadel of your soul. To get a better idea of the intended purpose of a dream sanctuary, let's turn to the definition of the word itself to concretize our relationship to it in terms of lucid dreaming.

A sanctuary is a place of refuge for those seeking safety. For your purposes, that safety entails having a stable space in a dreamscape that's unlikely to collapse. Your dream sanctuary is a sacred place of soul exploration. This is one reason you need to develop relationships with your spirit guides by reaching out with humility and warmth. Your spirit guides need to be needed, and this is one of the prime purposes of that need - to meet on the sacred ground of your dreams to benefit from the ancient wisdom offered by your spirit guides.

With all this in mind, it's time to focus on the space itself and the characteristics you want and need it to feature to make it work for you.

A Hiding Place

Due to its purpose, your dream sanctuary is somewhat set apart as a feature of lucid dreaming. This is a constant in your lucid dreamscape, and it may take you some time to feel adept enough to create the space as a stable manifestation in your lucid dreams.

By "pre-fabricating" it, you create an icon in your mind. The more stable it is in your mind, the more stable it will be in your lucid dreams. That's why detail is so important. Spend some time thinking about the kinds of spaces in which you feel both safe and nurtured. You might want your dream sanctuary to take the form of a cave in the side of a cliff face or a Bedouin-style tent. Whatever "safety" means to you is the first feature you should consider.

For example, think of the spaces that most attracted you in childhood. I remember sitting in the car as my family traveled to a nearby city. The highway's median was grass, with intermittent groves of coniferous trees, shrubs, and bushes at their base. As we passed these, I would always dream of how I might live in the groves. I imagined myself in a tent, layered with cushions and cozy Afghans. Another favorite space was the genie bottle in the television show I Dream of Jeannie. I always wanted to live in that bottle, with its exotic décor and plush cushions.

While childhood dreams may sound silly to adults, they provide us with clues about our psychological needs. An introvert, I was given to hiding as a child. I liked the idea of being in places that were in plain view and yet, offered invisibility. Take some time to think of your childhood hiding places and why you chose them. What did you go there to do? How did you feel when you were visiting them?

Meaningful Surroundings

Once you've arrived at your definition of safety and comfort for your sacred dream space, you must consider how you want the space to look. Remember this is "for keeps." The dream sanctuary is a static, stable place for a reason – this is where you know you can tackle the big questions, conversing with your spirit guides and discovering what they have to share with you.

I am a great believer in the power of color. This is especially important for your dream sanctuary, as the color tends to define the mood of a place. It sends a very strong message of intended purpose and ambiance. Choose colors that speak to you and understand the spiritual significance of the colors you're choosing. Color resonates and has a specific energy. Consider these colors and their spiritual meaning:

- **Green:** This is the color of the natural world, of balance and harmonious communication. It's ideal for a dream sanctuary in any shade.
- **Yellow:** Reason is at the heart of yellow, but it also represents fun, intellect, and personal power.
- **Orange:** This dynamic color is active, spurring productivity and creative solutions. NB: It may be a little "hyper" for a dream sanctuary.
- **Red:** Physically vital and passionate, the color red stimulates spontaneity but also signifies stability. Use this color but sparingly. It will assist in stabilizing the space but may interfere with communication if there's too much of it splashed about your dream sanctuary.
- **Purple:** This deeply spiritual color is ideal for the purposes of a dream sanctuary. Choose a jewel tone for your dream space to inspire intuition and the energies of the universe flowing through you.
- **Blue:** A shade of blue that's both rich and vibrant should complement your other colors both spiritually and aesthetically. Signifying peace, love, emotional profundity, and spiritual openness, blue is a natural fit for your dream sanctuary.

Whatever your favorite colors are, consider them in terms of the dream sanctuary's purpose and how you want it to work in your lucid dream state. Your colors should be chosen with care and then applied harmoniously, creating a space that pleases both your eye and soul and which supports the sanctuary's purpose.

Taking Care

Why is color so important to your dream sanctuary? All colors have spiritual resonance. All colors make us feel something. Color has power, and so does design. That's especially true when you're choosing colors for your dream sanctuary according to how they resonate with you and designing the space to your soul's unique needs.

As you progress with your dream sanctuary, it's important to think in terms of what you want. You're not conforming to a template of any kind, regardless of the practice's origin. You create precisely the space you need in the way you need to create it to stabilize it as a static element of your lucid dreams. You're creating this sacred space as a place to retreat to the needs of your soul with those entities most able to help you realize those needs. There can be no variance in the appearance of this space in your dreams. It must always be available to you in precisely the way it has been in any other dream. This is a soul space in lucidity that must remain stable and ready for you when you need it for the sake of counsel, discussion, answers to questions that arise in the course of lucid dreaming or in waking life. This is your lucid dreaming hub and a source of self-knowledge and healing in the company of your spirit guides, whether ancestors, archetypal presences, or random but strangely familiar people.

So, take care in selecting the elements of your dream sanctuary. Remember that you're designing a sacred space for your exclusive use. Valuing the holiness of your journey as a human means acknowledging the same holiness in your soul. Make sure you know you're worth it. If you can't say you know that, then you have some healing to do before you attempt any feat as complex, demanding, and revelatory as creating a dream sanctuary.

And that is, in no way, a bad thing. All in life is growth. The moment growth ends, death kicks in. Accidents notwithstanding, an absence of growth signals the imminent conclusion of human life.

This happens not because a life without growth has no value or is not "productive" (our modern obsession) but because the organism has begun to devolve, triggering systemic entropy. Whether through neglect, self-abuse or disease, an accident, terrorist attack, or in our sleep, we die. But when we die to all growth, we only go through the motions – the walking dead.

So, growing edges are also guides. We all have them, and we should all welcome them as the wonderful outfall of being these incredible speaking, cognitively advanced beings we are.

Home Is the Keyword

As you begin choosing objects and accouterments for your dream sanctuary, think of your physical home. Why do you love it? What about it reflects who you are and what you stand for? Do you feel nurtured within its walls?

These guiding questions will lead you to some essential truths about yourself, and they're not all aesthetic truths. Some concern your psychological framework, which will include a very clear template for what constitutes "home."

Think carefully about why you live where you do. Think about how you felt when you moved in and how you decorated it to reflect your taste. You have a favorite room. Picture it and discern what it is about this room that makes you feel safe and cared for as you spend time in it.

These are the elements that are most important to your dream sanctuary. In the realm of lucidity, physical comfort is less important but if physical comfort imparts a sense of calm and belonging in you, then include it in the furnishings. Make them plush and yielding. Create a womb for your soul, and its coming work with your spirit guides and ancestors.

This is your secret garden. Perhaps your dream sanctuary is a garden, alive with the rich scent of night-blooming jasmine (sensory details matter too). Or maybe it's a chaise or a funky collection of overstuffed chairs, with hand-crocheted Afghans over them. It doesn't matter.

What matters is that you create your ideal vision of calm self-nurture and that you understand, in your deepest core, this is your sacred space – inviolable and wholly yours throughout your life and perhaps, even beyond it. Never has a human yet returned to relate the tale.

The true gift of Shamanic practice is not in the adventurous aspect of its pillars but in its freedom. As humans, we are all joined in history, to places we've forgotten about and to belief systems we've allowed to wither in favor of more autocratically oriented ones. The freedom offered in Shamanism's ideas and practices is natural. It is not worked toward or earned. Freedom is the truth about humanity's relationship with Creation – how we live in it and die in it.

These ancient clues about ourselves are available to the open heart that understands the common threads of our human history. Shamanism has loaned lucid dreamers a fine model for the soul's development and healing in the dream sanctuary.

Rooted in the human creature's antiquity is the wisdom we know through a glass darkly, for the most part. Helped by lucid dreaming and a wider understanding of Shamanism's history, common to us all, it's my hope we all find the peace of sanctuary and a solution to our malaise in this world.

In our next chapter, we'll get down to discussing self-healing. I've touched on it, but we haven't had an opportunity to get into the nitty-gritty, so that's what Chapter 12 is for!

Let's discover more.

Chapter Twelve: Healing Yourself in the Dreamscape

I know that many of you will take a keen interest in this chapter. You've come to find something non-traditional to support your healing from any number of life's wounds. I applaud your openness and willingness to read about complementary approaches outside the realm of Western medicine.

This book is not intended to serve as a substitute to consulting your primary care doctor or mental health professional about a disorder, condition, or illness supported by such professional services. Please consult a doctor if you're concerned about your health. Healing requires expert support and spiritual/intellectual work, both as self-nurture and to move the spirit and body toward a place of true holistic wellbeing.

Healing has many connotations, though. Healing yourself in the dreamscape primarily addresses old wounds but, in so doing, often addresses the mysterious physical consequences of those psychic wounds. We have yet to agree about the extent to which events in the mind impact events in the body, but we know that emotional stress manifests physically in myriad ways. There are many other examples extant, including PTSD/CPTSD, which can be responsible for rendering numerous unpleasant physical symptoms, like headache, migraine, body aches, and muscle spasms.

As I've said above, this book is not a substitute for the advice of your primary care doctor or mental health professional. But I know that some of you reading will have been through traumas like chemotherapy and radiation, childbirth, orthopedic surgery, and other events which have taken a tremendous toll on your body. You have been through your medical treatment and are moving toward renewed health.

You're hoping that lucid dreaming can help. You'll be happy to hear that there's abundant evidence to support that hypothesis, so let's find out more about healing yourself in the dreamscape.

Promising Partners – Transpersonal Psychology

As it grows and advances, the study of dreams is increasingly becoming recognized as a partner to psychology. What could be more helpful to the discipline of psychology than the very ground of the human mind in dreams?

In the early 1960s, the field of transpersonal psychology arose, as advanced by Abraham Maslow. Transpersonal psychology invites human spirituality to the table, recognizing it as a component of the human-animal worthy of deployment as a tool by those seeking wholeness.

The word "transpersonal" means to move beyond our self-perceived isolation as humans to recognize not just the unity of all things but our place in that unity.

The transpersonal is very much alive in most traditional Faith systems yet drowned out by the personalization of the Divine-human relationship. Transpersonal psychology seeks to respond to that by bringing the human needs answered by various forms and conceptualizations of spirituality under the umbrella of psychology.

"Transpersonal psychology is concerned with the study of humanity's highest potential, and with the recognition, understanding, and realization of unitive, spiritual, and transcendent states of consciousness."

D.H. LaJoie and S. Shapiro

Definitions of Transpersonal Psychology, 1992

I find the ideas behind transpersonal psychology to be long overdue for wider dissemination and worthy of further exploration. The proposed partnership between the lucid dreaming and transpersonal psychology communities is very exciting because of the potential the union of these two areas of study represents. Our dreams, spiritual cores, and intricate minds are complex, under-examined information that promises insights that have eluded us over time. And part of that raft of information is how our minds, when directed to do so, may assist us in healing our psycho-spiritual wounds and even physical healing.

Natural Partners

In his 2018 article in the Journal of Transpersonal Psychology, Bridging Transpersonal Psychology and Lucid Dream Research, Tadas Stumbrys of Vilnius University recognized the power of a potential partnership between lucid dreaming and transpersonal psychology.

In writing the article, Dr. Stumbrys hoped to present to the TP community the advances seen in lucid dream research in recent years (including 2021, as we've explored earlier in this book). The goal is to re-establish a relationship with the discipline to the mutual benefit of both research and study communities.

The earlier collaboration between the two, Stumbrys contends, can be re-established to benefit both. His article also advances lucid dreaming as an expressly transpersonal experience, in which the dreamer, knowing she is dreaming, directs the dream and engages with it toward the desired result. As noted in the quote above, this is a transpersonal action, a "transcendent state...of mind".

Stumbrys also pointed out a stream of transpersonal interest in ongoing research since the separate development of lucid dreaming and TP and recognized the psychophysiological research trend of recent years in lucid dreaming (centering on Rapid Eye Movement in the sleep cycle). He made a strong case for the mutual benefit to the two areas of interest embodied by a partnership renewal.

As transpersonal psychology examines the role of the spirit and its operation within the "whole human being," the role of lucid dreaming in healing to restore genuine homeostasis, which includes the fullness of the human in body, mind, and spirit - a consubstantial and indivisible truth about our species – there exists a tremendous opportunity in the two spheres creating that magical Venn Diagram that signals understanding and an increase in human wellbeing.

In his article in the Lucidity Letter in 1991, Healing Through Lucid Dreaming, Stephen LaBerge reminded readers that sleeping and dreaming are naturally healing processes that the body engages in without prompting. So, lucid dreaming already resides in the body's self-healing space, along with the psychophysiological act of sleep and the conventional dreams that help us make sense of our lives.

Throughout the article, LaBerge cites the holistic nature of the human. As I've said above, homeostasis includes the mind and spirit. When one is out of balance, the rest of the organism is, as well. Just as breaking your little toe can wreak havoc up the physical chain, so can life setbacks, mental and physical malaise affect the whole.

LaBerge points out that the conventional dream, especially in the form of nightmares, points to reactions and behaviors emanating from us in response that need healing. He situates that healing in lucidity.

The dysfunction indicated by nightmares has a healing cousin in lucid dreaming. The ability to choose our reactions in the dream and direct the action gifts us with a forward. We are presented with an internal mechanism, available to us through the practice of lucid dreaming, of resolving conflict in our lives.

In our chapter on dream characters, I've talked a little about conflict resolution with hostile or threatening dream characters. This is an advanced technique, to be sure, but not inaccessible by any means to the determined practitioner. Those dream characters are acting out issues rolling around in your subconscious. Some of these issues you may have buried for a long time or only a short while. But hostile dream characters who appear randomly come with a gift for you - resolution of outstanding issues plaguing your subconscious. Reconciling with these characters is one form of the healing offered by lucid dreaming and skill to which you should aspire.

Essentially, LaBerge says that we are the masters of our own minds, with the practice of lucid dreaming as our healing conduit. In the lucid dream space, we are liberated to experience our deepest wounds (and those of lesser profundity) and heal them.

As I've said in the previous section, transpersonal psychology and lucid dreaming should again unite to explore and lift up lucid dreaming potential to heal. LaBerge's work (not just in this paper but in his career in this field) calls on them to recognize the urgency of that reunion.

The OMNI Experiment

In April of 1987, OMNI Magazine undertook a detailed study of lucid dreaming, led by Stephen LaBerge and Jayne Gackenbach, then of Sanford University and the University of Alberta/Athabasca, respectively and 1,000 study subjects. The study leads presented the results of the OMNI experiment in the Lucidity Letter in December 1989.

Results on healing were also noted, with the authors remarking that few participants associated lucid dreaming with healing. From the sample of participants who did think of lucid dreaming's potential for healing, 77% said they'd succeeded in employing it.

We'll talk briefly about the OMNI experiment when we arrive at a discussion of lucidity healing nightmares in the next chapter. For now, we'll discuss the experiment's results in terms of other types of healing.

Physical Healing Results

The OMNI experiment rendered some interesting results regarding this category of healing.

For the purposes of clarity in the experiment, "bodily healing" was defined as going to sleep with specific physical pain or discomfort and awakening to find it gone due to a lucid dream involving the pain being acknowledged and addressed.

But not all subjects enjoyed immediate pain reduction or elimination. For some, the process took several weeks or sometimes months, but they attributed the "healing" to the dream they'd experienced.

The OMNI experiment resulted in 8 such cases, divided evenly between the sexes. The average age of this sample was almost 37½ (in a range including subjects from the ages of 32 to 57). Of the eight subjects who reported being relieved of a physical complaint by lucid dreaming, 5 were frequent fliers, reporting one or more lucid dreams per week. Flying lucid dreams were also common to the members of this group.

One of the participants in the experiment recounted her dream, which addressed a thundering headache:

"Because of a terrific headache, I took a nap. While sleeping, I found the solution to the headache. I would chuck my head up in a lathe and turn the top of my head off. Solution found I couldn't wake myself up. I thought I had to wake up so I could solve the headache problem. Of course, when I did awaken, the solution was ridiculous, but the headache was gone!"

It should be noted that this experiment barely nods toward empiricism. People sometimes say the darndest things, and some of those things simply are not true. OMNI and its leads in the experiment had no means of controlling exaggeration among participants, for example. The veracity of participant statements is, therefore, only assumed – not verifiable.

It should also be clarified that none of the instances of healing claimed by participants in the 8-person group were addressing calamitous physical ailments. In all cases, these were physical wounds that were destined to "heal."

A Template

These accounts from participants indicate that it's possible for the lucid mind to influence events in the body – to an extent. For certain physical ills, solutions are in the mind of the dreamer on a limited basis.

Further, as the summary of results points out, several other commonalities at work underlines the hypothesis that lucidity may promote physical wellbeing in resolving minor ailments.

- All participants had a history of lucid dreaming. All were able to control their dreams, whether lucid or conventional.
- All went to sleep with a strong intention to eliminate the discomfort they were experiencing.

- In lucidity, that intention was recalled.
- Either the dreamer or a dream character acted to resolve the problem.
- Positive results were seen in the dream.
- Relief of pain/discomfort on awakening or at some time later.

Unfortunately, the results of the OMNI experiment rendered somewhat muddy results for varieties of healing beyond the physical. Still, this noble attempt rendered some worthy fodder for future research and study, and that's never a bad thing.

Look at the bulleted list just above. You can see that the commonalities of the 8 participants who recounted healing a physical ailment in their lucid dreams form the basic framework of dream induction at their very center. This is deeply encouraging for those seeking healing in the lucid dream space. It tells us there is a template of action related to intention, before and during the dream, as a key component of healing in the lucid dream space. This, I believe, applies to any type of healing.

The same template applies. The same intention applies. The same chain of events applies.

And at the heart of it all lies intention. The intention is the key to your successful employment of lucid dreaming as a healing tool. What this means, in practical terms, is that you resolve yourself to the solution. The intention is not wishy-washy. The intention is forceful. What is intended will be done. There is no space for equivocation in the realm of what we genuinely desire, and any deviation from intentionally pursuing it is where we fail.

Whether or not you're seeking physical, psychological, or spiritual healing, the template formed by the commonalities between the 8 OMNI experiment participants is applicable. The special sauce in this scenario is the intention and all that it implies in terms of your role as an active agent.

While it's easy enough to intend to address a raging pain in your head genuinely, it's perhaps a little less easy to address spiritual or psychological malaise. We tend to demonize such shadows on the soul when they really have no intrinsic negative value, except in the most extreme cases (psychopathy, Machiavellianism, sociopathy). While the immediacy of a headache gets our attention, we hesitate to address the needs of our soul and intellect.

Lucid dreaming, coupled with your willingness to name the problems you intend to address with its help, has the power to self-nurture on a deeper level. At the core of every human, this level determines more about the quality of our lives than we give it credit for, even in our advanced age of technological wonders and the ubiquitous Elon Musk.

With the application of the model which emerged from the OMNI experiment, there is a simple set of steps, recommendations, and explicit requirements that will assist you in navigating the dreamscape toward whatever type of healing you seek. With unshakeable intention on your tool belt and a mastery of your lucid dreaming space, you're halfway there. With honesty, openness, and the power of your invincible intention, OMNI shows us we have more control over the quality of our lives than we ever might have imagined. These eight people and their description of what their lucid dreams have in common have given us something of a gift – a user-friendly, uncomplicated roadmap toward a healing-empowered lucid dreamscape.

Throughout this book, we've discussed various strategies, contexts, and techniques for arriving at the state of lucidity and then, to do what we've come to that state of consciousness to do. Lucid dreaming asks of us a certain skill set. Stephen LaBerge and others in the field have created a variety of ways to nurture and foster these skills, guiding us toward the lucid state if we've never experienced it before and telling us how to improve our skills if we have.

Applying what you've learned and your progress toward an enhanced ability to stabilize, control the action, manifest, and interact will empower you. This will allow you to arrive at your goal, seeking healing through the life skill of lucid dreaming, a complex of skills that returns enormous rewards to those who practice it. Add to all you've learned so far in this book the power of intention, and you are well on your way to becoming adept in the land of lucidity and your own best friend in body, mind, and spirit.

You are the author of much of your own healing (with all provisos at the head of this chapter in mind).

Next, let's talk about nightmares and sleep paralysis and how we can overcome these problems in our sleeping life with lucid dreaming.

Chapter Thirteen: Overcoming Nightmares and Sleep Paralysis

"Sometimes, the wrong train can take us to the right place."

Paulo Coelho

Nightmares are the stuff of which nightmares are made! Many of us suffer terribly from them, disturbing our sleep, work, and relationships. The American Academy of Sleep Medicine defines nightmares as "...vivid, realistic and disturbing dreams typically involving threats to survival or security, which often evoke emotions of anxiety, fear or terror.

Nightmares have psychological origins, from stress, anxiety, and depression to old business from the past that's crying out for our attention or traumatic life events (PTSD). While only between 2 and 8% of Americans have regular nightmares, but the loss in productivity due to poor sleep quality amounts to more than $1,200 per worker per year. And at least some of that effect is attributable to nightmares.

Overcoming nightmares takes us back to the quote at the top of this page. We don't like nightmares. We want to rid ourselves of them so we can sleep soundly and well and function normally during our waking hours. But as we do so, the "wrong train" of nightmares can convey us to a destination that produces manifold results well beyond the elimination of these sleep-busting terrors.

We'll also talk about sleep paralysis in this chapter and how dreamers can address both problems helped by lucid dreaming.

Before we begin, I will offer the same proviso I did at the beginning of the previous chapter. The information in this book is not to be considered a substitute for consulting your primary care doctor or mental health professional when addressing serious issues like disabling phobias, anxiety, depression, tachycardia, or shortness of breath.

Nightmare Disorder

Nightmares are much more common in children. Their freshness to the world means that children are sorting through a reality they don't yet understand, and that process, in sleep, can mean vivid and frightening imagery. But as children approach adolescence, the frequency of nightmares reduces significantly.

Many people have occasional nightmares throughout their lives. But for some people, nightmares are frequent if they disrupt their lives and ruin their sleep quality.

To this day, there is no agreement in the medical and scientific communities about why we have nightmares. Those in the field of sleep medicine and their counterparts in the field of neuroscience can't even seem to agree about why we dream, never mind have nightmares.

One point of consensus is that dreaming helps us sort through our emotions and the events in our lives. Dreams also help us collate and solidify memories. It's believed (but there is no empirical evidence to this end) that nightmares serve a similar purpose but that they address trauma and anxiety encountered in daily life. We know that sleep deprivation, mental health issues, stress, trauma, and anxiety contribute to nightmares and certain prescribed medications and withdrawal from others (pain killers and tranquilizers, as these suppress REM sleep when nightmares occur).

Nightmare Disorder occurs when you:

- Encounter nightmares over four times a month
- When your sleep quality deteriorates, affecting your ability to function and your mood
- When your frequent nightmares coincide with starting a newly prescribed medication.

If this describes you, schedule a visit with your primary care doctor to talk about why you're encountering so many nightmares.

Desperate Times

There's no question that COVID-19, with its long-term isolation, prohibitions against public gatherings, and fear of catching the virus via physical contact, has proven to be difficult for all of us, wherever we live on the planet.

Add to the requirements of a pandemic – summed up as "keep your distance and keep your germs to yourself" – the avalanche of pseudo-scientific mumbo jumbo emanating from conspiracy theorists, virus deniers, and anti-vaxxers. To our anxiety was added the insult of misinformation.

The scale of this health crisis and the millions of people dead or sickened with long-term health implications and those who have only had their lives put on hold is megalithic. The denial of this reality seems almost cruel, with families in mourning all over the world.

But when isolated from one another, whether by distance, philosophy, or creed, it's so much easier for radical distrust to sneak in and make the distance between us more noticeable.

Humans are social creatures. We crave, in varying measure, the solace of other humans. So, quarantine requirements were borne with no little sorrow by most of us. We found some relief from that sorrow in electronic media, with its ability to connect people over vast distances. While somewhat comforting, that's nowhere near the same as time spent genuinely together.

The tremendous psychological effect of the isolation and disconnectedness alone were burdensome without the added weight of mendacious voices that, for whatever reason, wished to sow doubt that the pandemic was materially real. When this factor was added, anxiety was enhanced by a kind of shocked disbelief. Why would people go to such lengths to deny the reality we've all been struggling to live through?

I think it's important to discuss this factor in the context of nightmares because we will be feeling the repercussions of this pandemic for years to come. Those years will see a spike in mental health conditions as just one of the consequences of what's required by the unfortunate global dissemination of a deadly virus. While unavoidable for the sake of public health, the fallout from the isolating experience of quarantine will be making itself felt for some time.

An Urgent Need

According to an article in Scientific American in October 2020, COVID-19 has generated a global "dream surge." Any traumatic event will most likely change the dream life of those who experience it. But the global scale of these dreams, many of which are – if not nightmares – are, at the very least, bad dreams. Featured are hostile dream characters, sensations of being attacked, late, confined. From all over the world, what we've all been feeling is what we've all been dreaming.

In an increasingly complex, heavily populated, and interdependent world, there are bound to be more times like these in our collective future. And now, more than ever, humanity needs a friend to accompany it through such times. Lucid dreaming can help us heal the anxiety, depression, and desire to exit this life prematurely. It can help us learn to live with the kind of equanimity that our desperate times demand. And with all the trauma hanging in the air, it can help us transcend the discomfort of the moment to find shelter from the nightmares that plague us.

Let's discover how to overcome nightmares and take control of our inner turmoil.

Imagery Rehearsal Therapy (IRT)

A variety of Cognitive Behavioral Therapy, IRT, is being used to treat PTSD, encountering vivid, recurring, frequent nightmares as one of their symptoms. PTSD nightmares often return people to the site of their trauma. IRT's role is to reduce the frequency and severity of nightmares for PTSD patients by manipulating the way dream imagery is experienced.

Patients of IRT are started off with the least terrifying of the nightmares they're experiencing, then walked through the dream and the accompanying images by their therapists to "deconstruct" and reconcile with them and the incident they represent.

By starting with the least frightening nightmare, the patient is eased into the practice of revisiting the imagery without triggering a fear response. This builds patient trust and confidence.

Lucid dreaming is often used in conjunction with IRT therapy because the aim is to change the dream's narrative and, thus, change its imagery and the way patients experience it. Here's the process:

- If you've been experiencing nightmares, I hope you're writing them down in your dream journal. If you feel you need to start with the least scary, then do so. But if you'd prefer to start with the most recent one, even if scarier, you'll probably be more successful in breaking through. (If you are a PTSD patient, please talk to your therapist before attempting lucid dreaming).

- Write down every detail of the dream you can remember. Images should be recorded first, and then the emotions you attach to the images.
- Now, you're going to re-write the narrative. You're going to think carefully about the images and events in the nightmare and how you'd prefer those events to unfold. Concurrently, you will visualize the imagery of the narrative, applying the same detail you did to the original nightmare. Then, you'll apply the new emotional framework to the revised imagery.
- Once you feel confident, like an actor rehearsing lines, you will memorize your re-imagined nightmare and repeat it in your mind often. You will review the re-structured nightmare right before going to sleep.
- Remember that you may not succeed on your first try. The important thing is to concretize the new narrative in your mind so you know every detail of it, backward and forward.
- Apply intention. After reviewing your nightmare before sleep, say something like, "I will see this new vision."

Next, let's talk about sleep paralysis, what it means and how to deal with it.

Sleep Paralysis – Good and Bad

The word "paralysis," of course, has unpleasant connotations, so when we see the words "sleep paralysis," our initial response is horror.

But not all sleep paralysis is bad. Some sleep paralysis is nothing more sinister than a natural part of the sleep cycle, occurring in REM sleep. It's when this phenomenon occurs outside REM that it's a problem.

Often caused by conditions like narcolepsy, sleep paralysis may be experienced after a bout of heavy drinking, the result of sleep deprivation, or stress.

An experience of this type of problematic sleep paralysis occurs when the sleeper is aware, while either going into or leaving the REM sleep cycle, so most instances are experienced while falling asleep or waking up.

Sleep paralysis may come with physical sensations like choking or feeling pressure bearing down on the body and even hallucinations. Most episodes last a few seconds to a few minutes, with more serious occurrences lasting significantly longer.

Sleep Paralysis in Lucid Dreaming

At the beginning of this book, we discussed how lucid dreaming has now been observed to occur in NREM sleep. But as we also know, the best-traveled territory of the lucid dream is REM sleep.

For that reason, lucid dreaming is sometimes accompanied by sleep paralysis. This is usually short-lived, so long as the dreamer doesn't panic. Knowing that sleep paralysis is a normal part of the sleep cycle is comforting for lucid dreamers for that reason.

Comforting or not, those of you seeking lucidity must know this aspect of your journey. Muscle atonia (the physical manifestation of sleep paralysis) restores full waking consciousness. But in the lucid dreamer, the phenomenon is experienced differently due to the variance in state of consciousness. When you know you're dreaming, sleep paralysis is a known quantity. When you exit REM, directly engaging wakefulness, the effect can be frightening. That's because REM has not concluded, and yet, you are awake.

In fact, the electrical impulses from your brain required to operate your muscles are confused by the continuation of REM sleep. So, basically, sleep paralysis is when you blow a fuse!

Lucid dreaming can assist your brain in better understanding sleep paralysis and the nightmares sometimes associated with it. The real problem with this sleep difficulty is the REM stage of the cycle playing past the bell.

What's of note here is that both sleep paralysis and lucid dreaming are overwhelmingly associated with REM sleep.

Reclaiming Control

The advice I'll give you here is very similar to what we discussed earlier regarding nightmares. But there is another dimension to some of the possible causes of sleep paralysis. Let's eliminate these before going any further.

- Stress
- Excess alcohol consumption
- Sleep deprivation
- Jetlag
- Increased anxiety

Please review these possible causes of sleep paralysis to ensure that you're not provoking the phenomenon. Eliminating possible causes is like testing foods to determine allergies – necessary to get to the heart of the matter.

If we've now determined that you're neither narcoleptic nor encountering some lifestyle challenges that need managing, we can discuss revisioning any disequilibrium in your sleep cycle. We'll also talk about other factors you can work on toward eliminating the problem. That may be the reason your REM stage is hanging on into waking consciousness.

The first and probably most important element of moving on to sleep paralysis is eliminating the fear factor. This is the single greatest roadblock to stopping it. As we discussed above, finding the core of the problem is a matter of patience and reflection. You'll find it well worth your time and effort, as you'll be killing two or more birds with one stone.

Going back to RIT, reviewing either your least terrifying or most recent incidence of sleep paralysis is your first step. From there, follow the same steps with some key adjustments to address the presenting discussion.

- Instances of sleep paralysis should be recorded in your dream journal. If you've experienced them in the lucid state, they should be recorded in a separate section.
- Write down every detail you can remember. What physical sensations did you experience? Did you hallucinate? Did you float away? Describe what happened during your experience.
- Now, you will approach what you've experienced from a different angle. You're going to experience a pleasant physical sensation instead of the suffocation or shortness of breath you encountered.
- As you deconstruct and reconstruct your sleep paralysis experience, examine it against former traumas and sorrows in your life. Is there anything there that might indicate a forgotten or neglected source of the problem? This is a matter for you and your spirit guides to address in your dream sanctuary. They may have other ideas, as they've always been with you and have the 411 on unresolved issues.
- Like an actor rehearsing lines, you will memorize your re-imagined sleep paralysis incident and repeat it in your mind often. Once you feel confident, you will review the restructured experience right before going to sleep with the intention of applying your new perspective.
- Remember that you may not succeed on your first try. The important thing is to concretize the experience in your mind so you know every detail of it, backward and forwards.

• Apply intention. After reviewing your replacement sleep paralysis episode before sleep, say something like, "I will experience this differently."

The whole point of lucid dreaming is to experience the hidden, unknown parts of ourselves, and to find healing and self-development there. In that spirit, while the work involved may seem heavy now, imagine how you'll feel about it later – once you've been able to apply what you know to your own mind. Taking ownership of your whole self by taking control of the inner workings of your complex mind is an empowering act and one you'll be proud you pursued.

The OMNI experiment rendered 22 cases of lucid dreaming healing of nightmares, which amounts to 25% of the overall sample. This tells us there is genuine power in the state of consciousness experienced, especially when the dreamer has developed their self-awareness and ability to achieve lucidity.

As I've said, your ability is up to you. As you can see from what you've been reading, your methodology and commitment are a huge part of attaining lucidity and addressing persistent problems like nightmares and recurring dream paralysis – the bad kind, of course!

Get that dream journal ready! Our next chapter will address what to do when you wake up from your lucid dreams. But also, prepare to read more about common symbols and signs in lucid dreams and how to interpret them effectively.

Chapter Fourteen: Waking Up (and Making Sense of it All)

We've all awakened from dreams at some point in our lives, wondering, "What the heck was that?"

And that's a worthy question! Often, our dreams don't make a whole lot of sense - or at least any sense in our waking consciousness.

So, we will learn about some ways to ground ourselves as we emerge from REM sleep to help us retain more of our lucid dreams. In addition, we will review some of the most common symbols in dreams. These will help you, not only in your interpretative efforts but within the dream space. Recognizing these symbols and connecting them to your experiences in waking life is a powerful way toward healing and resolving outstanding, subconscious matters.

Getting Grounded

Getting grounded for the moment you wake up is a matter of preparation. Just as you prepare for lucid dreaming, you prepare for waking up from it.

A huge part of that process is on your night table – your dream journal. By keeping this book near you with a pen at the ready, you're empowered to record your dreams while they're still fresh in your mind. Just the physical action of writing concretizes your intention to remember your dreams in as much detail as possible. This is your first task of the day, and the more you do it, the more value the process will have for you – and the more likely you'll be to remember your dreams in detail.

Add to journaling a stated intention to remember detailed elements of your dreams. Say something like, "I will remember it all. I will remember it all in detail." Like reality testing (Am I dreaming?), making a statement about what you intend to do fixes the idea in your mind. As you repeat the reality testing question, you repeat the intention concretizing statement for the same reason. If the intention is powerful, then explicitly stated intention is even more so.

But there's much more you can do to shore up your morning memory of your dreamscape. One way you can do that is by is ensuring that you haven't neglected to make your sleeping area the most hospitable it can be to your purpose. Have you done that? Have you ensured that your bedroom is as comfortable and nurturing as it can be? If you've skipped over this step, I hope you'll reconsider your decision to do so.

And *you should* reconsider, because the ambiance is and comfort honor you and the dreams you'll be having. There is nothing "narcissistic" about self-nurture or comfort. These are, in fact, human needs. We all need these things, and we probably need them more if we're going to be lucid dreaming.

While you may think your sleep space is unimportant in relation to the lucid dreaming project, nothing could be further from the truth. So, at least a throw cushion and a stick of incense? Can I get that out of you?

Because another practice that can make remembering your lucid dreams and making sense of them easier – meditation and relaxation, finding your quiet center in waking consciousness right before bed is excellent preparation for lucid dreaming, and meditation achieves that. If that's not your style, though, you may want to enjoy a hot bath. Light a candle! Wallow languidly. You'll be asleep before you know it, having used your relaxing bath to prepare your mind for lucid dreaming. Pleasure is a wonderful prelude to lucid dreaming that works well for some practitioners.

Another key element of grounding yourself sufficiently to benefit from your dreams to remember them clearly is reality testing. All the reality tests you've read about are worthy, and by now, you've probably chosen your favorites. Use them regularly during your day. The more you call on reality tests, the more your brain will identify the question and understand its purpose. This will make you much more attuned to the content of your dreams as you're training your brain to recognize what you do to achieve lucidity. You're making it a partner.

Finally, preparing for lucidity and recalling its gifts demands at least a starting knowledge of dream symbols. I encourage you to seek information online and to compare it to your dream experience to discern the true meaning of dream signs and symbols. So, in the next section, we'll review some of the more common ones and their meanings.

Common Dream Symbols

We're now back in the land of the collective unconscious and its mysterious presence in the human mind. Dream symbols like Jungian archetypes and Shamanic practices reside in that unknown land that we have only begun to understand. In that land, there is a vast storehouse of shared experiences and attending information that is familiar and intelligible to virtually every human over the age of reason.

Something important to remember while we discuss dream symbols is that they will not reveal the meaning of your dreams to you independently. They're clues, and the meaning of their appearance can vary in ways peculiar to each dreamer. Universally, they hold the same meaning, but that meaning within personal contexts may take on another veneer or layer of significance.

A dream is like a Rubik's Cube that you can turn and turn and still not completely understand. But what we take from our dreams lucid and otherwise when we interpret them is invariably self-knowledge. There is nothing more intimate to us than our own bodies. The mind's role in that body is underexplored by so many people who could so richly benefit from having a closer relationship with it. That's one reason I've been itching to share what I've learned about lucid dreaming. In the Rubik's Cube puzzle that all dreams are, lucid dreams hold unique potential to know ourselves more fully and more fruitfully. And dream symbols are one of the most potent reasons for that, holding within them multiple interpretative possibilities, depending on the context they've appeared in. Common to us all, yet participating in our endless emotional, intellectual and spiritual diversity, these symbols hold tremendous value for lucid dreamers.

Teeth

At the very top of the "greatest hits" of dream symbols are teeth; teeth falling out, teeth biting, a floating smile, teeth found in various places – teeth.

Teeth falling out is the most common manifestation of teeth in dreams. This can be a little disconcerting for dreamers. But dreams about teeth (unless you've been in heavy rotation at the dentist's office) usually aren't about teeth at all.

Dreams about teeth are concerned with communication. Teeth dreams generally indicate a sense of the dreamer's not being heard by people important to them. Because the symbol indicates conversation, the dreamer may have some self-confidence issues that need to be addressed. They may also experience a reticence in the presence of people they're in awe of or who intimidate them in some way.

If you dream of teeth, examine yourself honestly. Ask if you haven't felt like you're on the short end of the stick recently. A dream of teeth may be telling you that you need to assert yourself.

School

The symbol of school is another popular one. I've had many dreams about school.

This symbol represents a life lesson – usually the one you're learning when you encounter it in your dreams. Reading this dream is a matter of understanding how it relates to the past, how the past is present in each day, and how the past informs the future.

Most school dreams see the dreamer in the context of their past academic life, be it in kindergarten or university. The dreamer finds themselves back at their old alma mater. Sometimes, dream characters correspond to old schoolmates, but often, they don't. In my dreams, nobody talks to me in the corridor as I vainly search for my class. I don't have my books!

My specific dream about this symbol has occurred at times in my life when I've encountered turbulence or disappointments. I've been compelled to learn from these times and their events and to transform them into knowledge to inform my future. This is the role of the school symbol – to urge you to continue stumbling forward as you learn the lesson before you. It comes to remind you what you've learned before and are learning again, exactly as you did as a child, in your teens, or as a young adult.

The context of the appearance of the school symbol in your dream will guide you to a better understanding of the lesson you're in the middle of learning.

House or Apartment

I have dreamed often of this symbol, with some recurring dreams in the mix. The House symbol is about who you are in a much larger sense than the superficial. The House represents your purpose, but the symbol has other meanings, each embodied by various rooms of the house. An empty house or apartment has another meaning, which is personal insecurity, whether financial or interpersonal. But this symbol may also mean moving forward or transformation.

An abandoned or empty house or apartment in poor condition and in need of serious renovations is a sign of disorder in your own life and resulting in internal chaos. This dream symbol should be paid close attention to, as "renovation" is the theme underlying that of the house/apartment symbol.

The attic of a house is a symbol of your intellect and your highest aspirations and vocation. The basement is your subconscious, hidden in darkness but available to those who seek its murky contents. These are obvious interpretations of these areas of a house.

A dream in which water suddenly rises in your house or apartment is another dream you need to pay close attention to. This dream is revealing a sense of being emotionally overwhelmed - drowning in emotions that you're unable to manage. This is a wake-up call to pay closer attention to your emotions, to name them, and to claim them.

But elements of the rooms in the house, the type of house it is, its environment, and its personal emotional content all have meaning besides the symbol itself, as do the furnishings, dream characters, and other potential symbolic factors.

Of course, we can't leave this symbol without acknowledging the significance of home to the waking mind - the core of our development as people. This is always the family home when it appears in your dreams. Usually, if your family moved around a lot, the house you see will be one momentous event in your life. It's in those events that you'll find the interpretation. Who is present? What is the time of year? When the past visits, it's usually about something going on in the present. The dream will offer you a historical analog, which means clues about how to proceed or how to address a problem in the present time.

To end this chapter, we'll look at common dream symbols representing a strong urging from your subconscious mind that something needs to change. These symbols should not be ignored. They're red flags breaking through to you for a good reason.

Flying

Flying in a dream is another symbol with multiple meanings. In my own dreams, both lucid and conventional, I have flown often. I am, in fact, a frequent flier! The context is usually that of escaping from something that's chasing me. In my case, it seems that these dreams relate to being overwhelmed or in need of greater autonomy. The sense of flying for me, personally, is related to my personal independence and ability to do the things I need and desire to do without interference. I had many such dreams while in a less-than-nurturing marriage.

Sigmund Freud, apparently obsessed with the male member, believed that flying dreams were about "defying gravity" (feel free to make any allusion you choose). Freud also believed that flying dreams were a male preserve. A man of his time, that's to be expected.

Today, we know better. We know that many women have dreams of flying (like me) and that our dreams are not about what Mr. Freud believed. Freud himself said, "Sometimes a cigar is just a cigar," and that is the case here. In this instance – flying – the cigar is not in the picture for many of us, for painfully obvious reasons.

Flying is one of the most compelling features of lucid dreams. One reason for that is the unnatural nature of human flight. Just ask Icarus! We are not intended to fly on our own steam. We require a conveyance to achieve the glory of flight. And so, flying in a dream is a tip-off as to our state of consciousness.

The first time I had a lucid dream, I took to the air. But that was not as simple a dream task as you might imagine if you've never encountered this symbol. Rather, my mind saw a need to fly, occasioned by a threatening circumstance. Once that need was identified, I began to run, knowing I would take off and fly if I ran fast enough. The first few times I did this, my waking mind broke through and woke me, as it realized that flying was an impossibility. But as time went by, I had more control, lifting off automatically, without having to run to gain momentum.

At the heart of understanding your flying dreams is noting what you can see. Is the sky blue and clear? What's down below? Is the landscape barren or on fire? All the little details of flying dreams help you relate them directly to your waking experience at the moment. And this is the true art of lucid dreaming – understanding the dream in the context of your life.

The most common interpretation of flying dreams is the human desire to transcend a circumstance and to break free of it. This can mean as many things as the act of flying itself, so take your time and write every detail you can remember in your dream journal, including the emotions you experience.

Being Buried Alive

As with a flying dream, a dream of being buried alive demands you sit up and take stock of what's going on in your life; the details of dreams like this, as I've said above, can lead you to solutions you might be ignoring. We all fear change, but it's time to embrace solutions when we're hosting dreams like this one.

Do you hate your job? How about your significant other? Trouble in paradise?

All things have their time. Everything in our lives will repeatedly change because that's the nature of life. We can control those changes by initiating them when required, or we can drag our feet out of fear and have them forced on us.

Life is impermanent. Nothing lasts forever, including us. And a dream of being buried alive is a red flag. It's telling us we need to move on, that we need to suck up our courage and get out of whatever is suffocating our potential and/or spirit and accept the changes that will free us from it.

Don't be afraid. Just don't ignore this dream and contextualize it carefully. Be sure that you're aware of areas you may have been leaving on the back burner too long, like a health issue, a bad relationship, or an unacceptable work situation.

Falling

When you dream of falling, whether from a great height or down a flight of stairs, it signals insecurity and an entrenched sense of inferiority that interferes with your ability to function optimally.

Falling dreams usually occur when we feel as though we're not on a solid footing in some way. We may fear job loss, relationship collapse, or a health condition. But whatever is plaguing us, we need to pay serious attention to dreams about falling. As with dreams of flying and being buried alive, this symbol is a red flag, alerting us to a situation we need to bring forward and resolve.

Another aspect of the "falling" dream symbol is people's tendency to nurture old wounds. We all do it. There are some life circumstances and traumas we find difficult to relinquish. They're almost like security blankets as they're so familiar to us.

What we hang on to may be a love long lost, a grudge, or a cherished belief that we know is no longer true for us but which we hang onto for dear life, as it's so familiar. A falling dream is telling you you need to let go of something to move forward. Whatever you're hanging onto, it's more like a millstone or an albatross than a security blanket. It weighs you down, and the symbol of falling is making that clear to you.

As always, the context, items, and characters in this dream (although there may be none or few of them) all require careful examination to understand what the dream has to tell you. But your honesty about your current life is the true key. You already know why you've had this dream, but you need to work through the interpretation steps to arrive at reconciliation and eventual elimination of the blockage.

The falling dream is letting you know that it's time to travel light by letting go.

In our next chapter, we'll talk about lucid art and writing and how lucid dreaming can enhance creativity, taking your chosen creative form to the next level.

Chapter Fifteen: Creating Lucid Art and Writing

Creativity is a prized component of the human-animal. We all have some of it, some more than others, and then, there are the few of us who are creative geniuses.

Not all creativity is about art or one of its many subsets, writing. Writing is its own art form, just as dancing or writing code is. Politics and the rhetoric that attends it is art. Designing a building or a dress or computer-generated graphics is art. I suppose, then, that I should define the term for our purposes.

For art, let's define the word as "creating representations in a variety of mediums and formats." So, visible art created by pen, ink, pencil, charcoal, ink, water, oil, or acrylic paints is our shared definition for the purposes of this book.

In this chapter, we'll discuss how we can create within the dreamscape, assisted by Dr. Clare Johnson, who wrote her doctoral thesis about writing in lucid dreaming. Dr. Johnson now conducts a variety of seminars that guide participation toward lucidity and its transformative power. Readers here to learn about how to manage nightmares will find Johnson's book on the subject – entitled The Art of Transforming Nightmares – to be of great value.

The Hidden Wellspring

As I've said above, we're all creative. Whether we believe that or not, the human animal's creativity is boundless. We've created incredible advances toward bettering humanity like medicine, technology, and psychology. We've developed complex political systems and religious ideologies, and all these innovations have resulted from human creativity, for better or worse.

Within us, all is a tremendous wellspring of creativity secreted in our subconscious. In this boundless, hidden source lies the courage our conscious minds often deny us – the courage to create from our unique visions in the multifarious ways humans do.

Far too many of us restrain our creativity for whatever societal norm we've been told we must conform to if we want to succeed and live out our potential as humans. We're told our ideas are crazy, that our creations are hideous and that we have no talent. And we take those negative messages to heart, sitting on our innate creativity for the sake of the perspectives of others.

That self-defeating reality is much more common than you think. Lucid dreaming, though, offers a means of recovering and reviving the creativity we've forgotten about. Buried under all the negatives messages and discouragement, the wellspring is still there, and lucid dreaming can help us access it.

Lucid Writing

One of Dr. Johnson's key findings in her Ph.D. thesis, The Role of Lucid Dreaming in the Creative Writing Process, was that the process of lucid writing begins in waking consciousness and the dreamer's approach to it.

Dr. Johnson began teaching Lucid Writing in 2005. She discovered there was obvious propulsion of creativity in the writing process to be had in lucid dreaming. This propulsion (the subconscious contributing) also birthed original ideas that sprang directly from the lucid state of consciousness. Dr. Johnson adapted what she learned as an approach to the treatment of nightmares.

Lucid writing results from a change in the imagery our subconscious generates. Creativity is not the only wellspring in the neighborhood of the subconscious. It's also the wellspring of the blockages that hold us back in life, like anxiety about worst-case scenarios and expecting the worst possible outcome. This is the wellspring in which you'll find neuroses and performative victimhood.

Creative writing sets us free from these hidden enemies, releasing the free-flowing creative energy we had as children. In lucid dreaming, the fantastic is accepted as what is. While this factor tells us we're dreaming, the fantastic and outrageous in lucid dreams are tailor-made for the creative writer. There is no judgment in lucidity. There are only the contents of the wellspring of creativity, which explode from the subconscious as we connect with it.

The Technique

Dr. Johnson's personal experience of lucid writing is striking. As her own most prolific subject, Dr. Johnson discovered a "zone" of unbridled, unforced inspiration in what she calls "the zone."

Her technique is simple. With paper and pen at the ready, close your eyes and relax your breathing. Choose an especially vivid lucid dream from your repertoire. Recall it in detail, including the emotional content, the information about the symbols you encountered in it, and the dream characters. Re-tell yourself the story, re-visualizing the dream (like a film in your head).

This process should produce a similar intellectual ambiance to that of lucidity, in which imagery begins to flow independently from the ground of the dream you're recalling.

The thoughts and emotions (and even the objects) you experience in the lucid state change rapidly. They morph into other thoughts and emotions, building on the previous ones and moving in unanticipated directions. The imagery will also transform. Don't hang onto any original version. Let it go. Let it morph into what it's going to be and then into what it will be after that.

As this process continues, you will be writing down what you see, think, and feel. Write every detail that occurs to you as quickly as you can. Capture as much of what you experience as possible. Even if what you write doesn't make perfect sense, that's not the point. What you're writing is an experience in real-time. You are creating a framework of the dream's contents to which you'll add walls, doors, windows, plumbing, and HVAC later.

If you're a writer, you'll know that often, stray thoughts come to you as the nubs of ideas for writing you're working on or plan to work on. Those stray nubs can even form the basis for an entire book!

What you write in the waking lucid dream state (which is unique and on the peripheries of lucid dreaming, according to Dr. Johnson) may seem odd, but don't judge it. Write it, then read through afterward, and you'll find that what you've written is much less "odd" than you'd believed. Your job is to build upon it as you write, in precisely the same creative process you take with the stray nubs we just talked about - ideas in their raw state. Johnson refers to this technique as "the writer's trance."

Your Inner Rembrandt

Dr. Johnson's presentation to the PsiberDreaming Conference of the International Association of the Study of Dreams in 2011 offers an alternative for those seeking their inner artists.

Many of us may have the desire, but we fear scrutiny, doubting our capacity to create art. There is an element of creation for public consumption, which is terrifying due to its self-revelatory nature. There is no such thing as creativity that does not, in some way, generate a response. We fear the negative response. We know from experience that it has the power to knock us off course in our creative journey.

Temporary art is a great way around that because what you're creating is ephemeral, not permanent. No one needs to see it but you.

Using sand in a tray, add a few objects to represent a recent lucid dream of your choice. Choose objects that reference or stand in for items in the dream-like furniture, buildings, people, dream symbols, and other features of your dream. By recreating your dream, you're not only enjoying the benefit of further analysis that may be even more revelatory than what you've written in your dream journal, but you're also creating art generated by your dreams.

Other temporary art mediums might be Play-Doh or an Etch-A-Sketch - specifically made for the temporary art of children. And if you like what you've created, you can take a photo. And (why not), maybe post it on Facebook for a select group of friends to see. This is how we come out of our creative silos - by seeing the merit of our own creations and sharing them with first a few, then more, and then, still more people.

Artists, both budding and established, find in the lucid dream space disinhibition and free space for experimentation. They find in the dream space inspiration and the absence of criticism – especially their own!

There is no critic more baldly sadistic than that of the creative person. The inner critic is an insistent voice in the mind of creatives, ever gnawing away at the artist, the writer, or the rhetorician, telling them, "You're an imposter!"

And lucid dreaming silences this unpleasant and corrosive voice, freeing us to splash paint and words and whatever else we're creating around with wild abandon.

Just as children thrive in their creativity, not giving one fig what anyone thinks of their creations, adult artists and dabblers in art alike can find total freedom in the lucid dream space. When very young, children create art that often bears little resemblance to reality, indicating a lack of concern for conformity in that regard. This is the creative spirit of some of the most celebrated artists in the world – those who go beyond and around, over and under whatever the prevailing artistic wisdom is. Children don't care how things "should" look. They see them from their own unique perspectives, telling us a uniquely point-of-view artistic tale.

And this is the naïvely powerful brand of art that lucid dreaming can help you achieve.

Lucid Dreaming Is the Creator's Best Friend

No matter what you're creating, lucid dreaming is your best friend. Because in lucid dreaming, you're in contact with the most profound depths of who you are. All the little nuances of life can be found in lucid dreams – things you've forgotten, neglected parts of yourself, the potential hidden in your self-consciousness – all these are available to you in conventional dreams but become more vivid and immediate in lucidity.

Because the unconscious, usually unavailable to you in waking consciousness, is at your disposal, the creator has unlimited access to its contents. And these contents are often inspirational and surprising to those who delve into them.

A study conducted in 2014 at Randolph-Macon College and subsequently published in Impulse, a journal of the Appalachia State University, explored the relationship between creativity and lucid dreaming.

The study employed pre-sleep autosuggestion to increase the chances of participants experiencing a lucid dream. The study leads suggested this period be extended for ongoing research to test the effects of autosuggestion on successively reaching lucidity over time.

The study assessed participants based on the presence of convergent creativity (applying logic – facts provided and answers/solutions) and divergent creativity (applying the imagination – a question spawns ideas/solutions).

The study concluded that creativity was not a prerequisite for lucid dreaming. It also found, of participants implicated, that only one could learn how to lucid dream (remembering that the study duration was a scant seven days). It was also found that the age of participants implicated was a contributing factor to the ability to learn to lucid dream.

Interestingly, research leads had no outside connection to the lucid dreaming community and thus took a purely dispassionate look at the subject from the standpoint of the neurological realities in play.

The conclusion they reached, namely, that testing cognition and its functions might lead the way to create a framework for more widespread induction of lucid dreaming. For those who've found lucidity to be elusive, this is hopeful news. The final word of these researchers is that studies of longer duration are required to see how testing and subsequent training might work together to improve access to lucid dreaming. Another conclusion is that more information about subjective consciousness (our awareness of our state of consciousness) could be gathered from similar, more in-depth studies.

Scores for divergent (imaginative) creativity were seen to increase substantially with lucid dreaming, which may challenge the perception of researchers that creativity does not make lucid dreaming easier. But the same was true for divergent (logical) creativity – lucid dreamers scored higher on this measure. And so, the aggregate of the two modes of creativity showed a substantial increase in those who experienced lucid dreams during the study.

Again, it's important to note that no researchers harbored a vested interest in the study's findings. For that reason, I've included this study's results, as it's clear that they offer the lucid dreaming community some vital information. When our personal opinions are removed from the mix, the art of lucid dreaming is still one which carries a genuine opportunity for the creative mind, whether imaginatively or logically based.

That means that all creators (whether painting a masterpiece or constructing a new healthcare system for the USA) can benefit from lucidity. Lucid dreaming is a friend to those who paint, write, sculpt, plan cities or write legislation, as per the study's findings. While not spectacular, the results of this study are rendered more hopeful by the dispassionate approach of research leads with no connection to or vested interest in lucid dreaming or its proponents.

That's something to sit up and take notice of.

Your Creative Journey

Whatever corner of creativity you're seeking to enhance with lucid dreaming, whether logic or imagination-based, making it part of your creative journey is, without doubt, a game-changer.

As the study discussed above demonstrates, there is emerging evidence to support further research in the scientific community into how lucid dreaming improves creativity. Even with results this inconclusive, it's clear that there is an effect in the lucid dream space that heavily influences creativity moving forward.

When we dream lucidly, we unpack the secreted fullness of our minds and what's lurking in them. There's no question that the contents of our unconscious/subconscious mind are a storehouse of unknown riches. The ability to unlock those creative riches with lucid dreaming can only be seen as a benefit to creators.

As researchers stated as one of the results arising, this minor study highlights the need to more stringently control the sleep settings in play and the training and testing of subjects implicated. That finding alone cries out for the research community to respond with a more stringent model carried out over an extended period. Will extending the time frame for autosuggestion, training, and testing of participants render even more encouraging results?

While that remains to be seen, only this kind of research can raise the clinical profile of lucid dreaming as support to human life in multiple areas, from creativity to nation-building to relationships, too. The sky's the limit.

In our final chapter, we will review some benefits of lucid dreaming. These benefits are numerous and compelling.

Chapter Sixteen: Improve Your Life with Lucid Dreaming

Before I leave you, it's important that you know what lucid dreaming can do for your life and overall wellness. We've read quite a lot about the subject now that the book nears its end, but this chapter is for reminding you that lucid dreaming has a distinctive role to play in improving your quality of life.

Remember: learning to lucid dream is a process and a journey. For most, it happens with a certain amount of effort. As you've read, your brain needs to be trained for lucidity, and that requires your steadfast commitment if you're to get to the land of lucidity!

Nothing more achieving was ever achieved overnight, in a month, or even in a year. Lucid dreaming is a long-term project in which you are the major deciding factor. Your dedication and readiness for lucidity are the most crucial factor in your success. So please be straight with yourself and make sure you're giving your efforts all the intentionality they'll need to get you there. And once you've arrived, here are some of the eventual and highly probable benefits you'll enjoy. Again, your alertness to changes in your thinking and behavior, your commitment to change, and your attentiveness to the journey are major contributing factors to fully enjoying these benefits.

Anxiety, Depression, and Psychosis

Just over 18 % of the US population suffers from some form of anxiety. That's a sizable chunk of the population, amounting to now fewer than 40 million people, while over 16 million suffer from some form of depression. Psychosis, while seen in only a fraction of the population, is a serious social challenge, as it represents a mind lost in an alternative reality.

For many reasons, these three disorders represent a public health emergency, among all the ills that attend them, including criminality, family dysfunction, lost productivity, and the social damage that occurs when all is not well with all of us.

A study appearing in Frontiers in Psychology in 2020 found that lucid dreaming has enormous potential for reducing anxiety and depression and a significant effect on nightmares stemming from conditions like CPSTD/PTSD. This isn't surprising as the study was conducted over a scant three months – a fraction in the long-term nature of treating post-traumatic stress.

The study, Neurobiology, and clinical implications of lucid dreaming explored the role of lucid dreaming from the standpoint of the REM stage of the sleep cycle. Psychosis, in this neurobiological sense, has something in common with REM sleep, as both generate subjective perception and the absence of rationality. But there the parallels end, as psychosis is a condition in which dreams (the subconscious) invades waking reality, challenging the model of reality the person experiencing psychosis lives in. Lucid dreaming is a state of consciousness specific to sleep.

But for all the conditions noted in this section, the study leads concluded that lucid dreaming was an effective addition to the psychotherapeutic toolbox, including to treat recurring nightmares.

As part of the conclusions of the study, Imagery Rehearsal Therapy is suggested (without being mentioned). Researchers name three ways that lucid dreaming can benefit those living with psychological disturbances like depression, anxiety, and psychosis (and resulting nightmares):

- By waking up
- By rationalizing there is no genuine threat to the extent (in the dream space or otherwise)
- By changing the narrative (!) of the nightmare/dream

The study's research leads clearly calls for strategic renewal in the treatment of nightmares and the disorders that provoke and boost the efficiency of lucid dream induction techniques.

The study also holds out hope for the understanding and treatment of psychosis with the support of lucid dreaming. Because of lucid dreaming's rarefied status as a unique state of consciousness, researchers believe that accelerated study of the phenomenon and research into its neurobiological underpinnings may reveal new information about the nature of consciousness and disturbances to it, which we characterize as mental illness.

Motor Skill Rehabilitation – Learning New Skills

We've spoken about the power of visualization earlier in this book and about the fact that if you can imagine yourself doing it, you're not far from doing it in the flesh, blood, and whatever other medium is active in the scenario.

The study acknowledges this truth as fact – a scientific study. Part of its conclusion is that lucid dream has the potential to improve skills training, the rehabilitation of motor skills, and sports performance.

By repeatedly imagining the contract of muscles, skills (and enhancement of existing skills) can be improved without performing the actual movements or knowing the rationale for performing them.

This reality is tremendously hopeful for the physically challenged, offering them to rehearse motor skills safely in the lucid dream state to be used in the waking state. This is also a means of testing the efficacy of lucid dreaming to reduce symptoms limiting mobility and the performance of fine motor skills.

A key finding of this study is one we should all be very interested in. During lucidity, performing any physical task or the rehearsal of motor skills saw a distinct spike in sensorimotor cortex activity in the brain. This effect is made possible by neuroplasticity.

The brain can rewire itself when stimulated. The more we do a certain task, the better at it we become. That's what neuroplasticity means – that practice makes perfect. This is as true of training for athletic events as it is for running heavy machinery or typing. The brain rewires when the action is repeated with regularity.

In lucidity, the state of consciousness more closely resembles the waking state. Therefore, rehearsal of physical activities in dreams benefits from an enhanced neuroplastic effect, present in lucidity.

This is an encouraging result that speaks of the intimate mind-body relationship and how the mind influences the performance of physical activities, even in a rehabilitative framework or one of seeking improved performance.

This result also tells us that lucid dreaming, with the right intention and preparation, can be the site of learning completely new physical skills through simple, self-generated imagery alone. Learn to ski? How about flamenco dancing? Any motor skills you desire learning are at your disposal once you've learned the fine points of lucid dreaming. There is no barrier to such life-enhancement, according to this study.

Equanimity and Emotional Control

If you've read this book closely, you'll see that I've offered numerous ways of looking at lucid dreaming as a means of getting at what's squatting in your subconscious, rent-free. Whatever that is for you, lucid dreaming is a framework for affecting a hasty eviction.

The subconscious becomes an accessible font of information with lucid dreaming. As you learn to control your mind, you learn to control your emotions. And control of your emotions is one pillar of emotional intelligence.

Having the grace to hold back when you feel like going off the rails is a sought-after life skill that few of us can boast of - not with any reliability. Most of us lose control of our emotions here and there. But the leaders of this world, who all boast enviable EQs (an indicator of emotional intelligence), know that leaders don't have the luxury of wearing their emotions on their sleeves. They model a trait called "equanimity."

Equanimity is the ability to take the negative moments of life with the positive moments without distinction. Every moment, regardless of its emotional content, has the strength of counsel. Every moment has value. Every moment can teach and build.

The Stoics of Ancient Greece based their philosophical contentions on this trait, similar in intent to "detachment" in Buddhism. Equanimity simply means that when life goes south, you remain rooted in the truth that the wheel turns, that life is sometimes difficult, and, without rancor, keep putting one foot in front of the other.

Lucid dreaming is a way of communing with the deepest core of who you are, deconstructing previously unknown narratives either holding you back or propelling you into unwanted mental health consequences like anxiety, stress, depression - even psychosis. Because of the access lucid dreaming grants you to the unconscious narratives, memories, and submerged memories of the past, there is great potential in gaining from your lucid dream journey the cherished trait of equanimity.

There is nothing more valuable to a human walking this battered planet than the equanimity that helps us live with integrity, neither fearing nor decrying its caprices and vagaries.

Improved Problem-Solving and Enhanced Creativity

Life presents us with problems. Most of us don't boast the measured emotional lives (equanimity) to cope with them when they arrive and we might. We flail. We rail against the unfairness of it all, and then we wrack our tired brains for solutions.

But in lucid dreaming, we have a constant friend. Just as we sometimes visit a sage friend to toss around potential solutions, the problem-plagued among us may turn to lucid dreaming for the answers their seeking.

While lucid dreaming is, by no means, a Magic 8-Ball, it is a source of clues, at the very least. From those clues, we can extrapolate the resolutions we seek. From dream symbols, dream characters, conversations, and counsel with our spirit guides and narratives that come to us to teach (from our own subconscious), we can find a way forward helped by lucid dreaming.

Sometimes, we may even get the answer we're seeking, disguised as a symbol or an even or dream character from our waking past.

Lucid dreaming also serves to impart the creativity we need to seek the answers to our problems. The clues we receive in our lucid dreams are nothing without our personal interpretation of them. This brings us to the power of creativity in the art of life.

We've talked about lucid art and writing in Chapter 15, but art and writing are also vehicles for solving problems. Creativity is a life skill as much as it is the euphoria of catharsis (the release of tension experienced when confronted with art, as in the theatrical art form of the Greek Tragedy). When creativity is enhanced, problem-solving is commensurately served. All the complex modes of thought that apply to the creation of art apply to the creation of solutions. A larger picture demands a detail-oriented eye to tease out the constituent parts. It's in these components of both art and problems that the masterpiece lies: the elegantly conceived solution.

That seems to me that the link between creativity and problem-solving is one of the greatest gifts of lucid dreaming. If dreamers can mindfully mine the subconscious contents, pulling it from it the monkey wrenches in the workings of their brains, they're also able to affect profound change in their lives.

We're learning more about problem-solving and creativity in lucid dreaming, but it isn't easy to apply optimal empiricism with most of the research work being done within the community. The personal proximity of researchers to the subject – as it does in any clinical setting – has an impact. However, without research being generated by this community, there is little opportunity for cross-disciplinary input and enlargement of the themes being researched.

Again, a partnership with transpersonal psychology would do much to alleviate this roadblock in the realm of research into lucid dreaming. But neurobiology and neuro-science, in general, can also play a role in the study of lucid dreaming. As the field continues to develop and gather significant public interest, I hope these partnerships and external sources of empiricism will teach us so much more about the scientific underpinnings of lucid dreaming and the role it might play in humanity's continuing health.

Improving the Life of Humanity with Lucid Dreaming

I believe that lucid dreaming will transcend the ongoing, sensationalized status it currently "enjoys" in the public consciousness. With increased research and study outside the lucid dreaming community itself, much more will be learned about it, and with more knowledge comes a superior empirical foundation. With that foundation in place, induction techniques will be improved, and the art of lucid dreaming will become accessible to many more people.

And that can only be a good thing. The collective unconscious is real. It's part of who we are as humans. Supported by lucid dreaming and the work of scientists, psychologists, neurobiologists, and a host of other professionals, we're standing on the brink of incredible potential for humanity in the untapped possibilities presented to us by lucid dreaming.

If lucidity can effect such changes in individual lives, what can it do for us, collectively? What would happen if billions of us were lucid dreaming all over the world? How would the wounds the collective unconscious has suffered over time be healed, and how would that healing lead to other changes.

Could a healed collective unconscious heal this planet, our home? That's a tremendous question. And it's a mighty thought.

For the time being, we must content ourselves with becoming the change we want to see in the world helped by lucid dreaming. Healing, learning, evolving, and connecting to our most obscure psychological corners. The sooner we get started, the better.

Bonus Chapter: Lucid Dreaming Checklist

To help readers get off to a flying start, I've aggregated key information in this book about your lucid dreaming adventure here in this checklist. In this section, you'll find the most important points about lucid dreaming and how to achieve it, and supporting actions that will boost your effectiveness.

- Intention is a keyword in lucid dreaming. What you genuinely intend to do, you will do. But when you transform an intention into a statement, it gathers more power and efficacy.
- Lucid dreaming has been practiced throughout human history. There is nothing novel about it.
- You cannot get "stuck" in lucid dreaming.
- You needn't be a spiritual adept at practicing lucid dreaming.
- Lucid dreaming does not provoke negative mental health consequences.
- The more information you have at your disposal, the more confident you'll feel about achieving lucidity

- A dream journal is an absolute must. Always keep it at your bedside. It's the first thing you should reach for in the morning when you wake up! And don't forget the pen!
- Prepare your physical space to make it:
    - **Comfortable**
    - **Dark**
    - **Quiet**
    - **Reflective**
- Remember – your bedroom is for sleeping and dreaming. No blue light in your sleep space. No television, no scrolling on your mobile device, no Kindle, no laptop.
- Train your brain with a variety of tools, like:
    - **Binaural Beats**
    - **Meditation**
    - **Visualization**
- Remember – you are individual; different techniques and methods work for different people. If one induction technique doesn't work for you, perhaps another will or a combination of methods may be what you need.
- The same goes for reality tests. Whichever one you choose must be the one you feel most comfortable and confident about. Try them all until you find the one (or a combination) that works best for you:
    - **Wake Back to Bed (WBTB)**
    - **Impossible Movement Practice (IRT Works Best in Conjunction with WBTB)**
    - **The Counting Technique**
    - **Mnemonic Induction**
    - **MILD (Rescript, Rehearse, Remind)**
- New dreamers are encouraged to build up their skillset by choosing the easiest way forward. For example, conflict is not be resolved. Leave the scene of any conflict that may arise with

a dream character by spinning or "flying" within your dream. When you have more experience, you'll be ready to rumble!

- Several methods can prevent lucid dream collapse:
    - **Spinning**
    - **Physical Touch**
    - **Focusing on a Physical Detail**
    - **Simple Math Problems**
    - **Staring at the Ground**
    - **Shaking Your Head**
    - **Focusing on Your Breathing**
- Don't expect time to behave the same way in lucid dreaming. It has little meaning in any dreamscape, whether conventional or lucid.
- Prepare yourself for the dream body by understanding your own body and its limitations more fully. Connect with your physical self to transcend it by choosing a form of movement to integrate your body and mind.
- Don't forget that reality checking is always there to help should things get "weird."
- The three-step method for spawning objects in lucid dreams:
    - **Focus Deeply on an Object That's Very Familiar to You to Start**
    - **Explore Your Emotional Connection to the Object**
    - **Choose the Right Environment for the Object by Visualizing it in Detail**
    - **Believe That the Object Will Manifest When You Dream**
    - **Repeat This Three-step Process Throughout the Day Before a Lucid Dream Session to Stamp the Intention to Spawn the Object on Your Mind**
- Learn the Jungian archetypes regarding dream characters to recognize them when they appear in your dreams.

- Remember that dream characters may not always be known to you or maybe hostile. You can't always control who shows up.
- Develop the skill to negotiate with dream characters over time to neutralize possible hostilities. These are most likely problems within you seeking a solution.
- Your dreamscape (landscape in the dream) can be whatever you want it to be but start small. Regularly revisit your dreamscape while awake to memorize its details and to concretize it in your mind to spawn it in the lucid dream.
- Contacting your spirit guides demands tremendous respect. Do so only when you feel confident enough to invite them to your dream space. Remember – they're not interventionists. They may appear to you, but they won't intervene unless you request it.
- Your dream sanctuary is a static presence. It is entirely within your control. Take your time to build it in detail.
- You and your spirit guides can only meet in the dream sanctuary if it is stable.
- Your dream sanctuary is your home in the lucid dream. This is the sanctuary of your soul, your spirit, your mind.
- Healing in the lucid dream space has limitations. Lucid dreaming is no substitute for consultation with your primary care doctor and/or your mental health professional.
- Image Rehearsal Therapy can help you overcome nightmares. You change the outcome of your nightmare by transforming the images and their meaning. The same is true of sleep paralysis. You set the intention to transform the nightmare/paralysis experience by revisioning it.
- Not all sleep paralysis is "bad." Most SP is a perfectly normal part of the REM portion of the sleep cycle.
- Ground yourself when waking up from a lucid dream by:
  - **Writing in Your Dream Journal**

- Meditating Before Bed
- Using Reality Tests Throughout the Day to Signal Your Brain That You Will Remember Your Lucid Dream
- Your Intention is Everything

• Lucid writing and art can be achieved by summoning your lucid dreams in the waking state, inducing the ambiance of the dream without calling on the state of consciousness.

• Lucid dreaming's benefits include:
- **Reduced Anxiety**
- **Reduced Depression**
- **Reduced Psychological Disturbance**
- **Enhanced Equanimity**
- **Improved Problem-Solving**
- **Greater Emotional Control**

Increased Creativity – Extending to every area of your life (see problem-solving) and not limited to artistic creativity.

Lucid dreams set you free to live your life to its fullest potential for happiness, satisfaction, and success. Learning how to leverage lucidity as life support is one of the most positive things you can do for yourself and the integrated health of your body and mind.

References

Horton, C.L., 2020, Key Concepts in Dream Research: Cognition and Consciousness are Inherently Linked, but do not Control "Control"!, Front. Hum. Neurosci. 14:259

Nieminen, J.O., Gosseries, O., Massimini, M., Saad, E., Sheldon, A.D, Boly, M., Siclari, F., Postle, B.R., Tononi, G., 2016, Consciousness and cortical responsiveness: a within-state study during non-rapid eye movement sleep, Scientific Reports, 6: 30932

Crookes, D., 2021, Can our brains help prove the universe is conscious?, Space.com

Hess, G., Shredl, M., Goritz, A.S., 2016, Lucid Dreaming Frequency and the Big Five Personality Factors, Sage Journals, research article, sourced online

Baird, B., Castelnovo, A., Gosseries, O., Tononi, G., 2018, Frequent lucid dreaming associated with increased functional connectivity between frontopolar cortex and temporoparietal association areas, Scientific Reports number 17798

Moutinho, S., 2021, Scientists entered people's dreams and got them "talking" Science Magazine

Papachristou, C., 2014, Aristotle's Theory of 'Sleep and Dreams' in the Light of Modern and Contemporary Experimental Research, Thessaloniki, Greece, E-LOGOS, University of Economics

Keevak, M., 1992, Descartes' Dreams and Their Address for Philosophy, Philadelphia, PA, Journal of the History of Ideas, University of Pennsylvania Press

Wright, D., 2011, Did Alleged Arizona Shooter Jared Loughner Think He Was Dreaming During Attack?, ABC News (An excellent example of exploiting lucid dreaming in popular culture to attracts viewers).

Blanke, O., 2018, Out of body experiences and their neural basis, London, UK, BMJ, British Medical Association

Nielson, T., 2020, The COVID-19 Pandemic is Changing our Dreams, Scientific American

Scott, M., date unknown, Dreaming Awake (Shamanic dreaming), The Blog for thoughts, ideas and random acts of radicalism

Spoormaker, V.I. and van den Bout, I., 2006, Lucid Dreaming Treatment for Nightmares, a Pilot Study, Basel, Switzerland, S. Karger AG

Albert, J., Houle, K., Kalasinski, S., King, J., Washington, S., Clabough, E., 2014, Exploring the relationship between creativity and lucid dreaming, Boone, NC, Impulse: the Premier Undergraduate Neuroscience Journal, Appalachia State University

www.ingramcontent.com/pod-product-compliance
Lightning Source LLC
Chambersburg PA
CBHW050510240426
43673CB00004B/172